AMERICA

The Judgment of Sodom and Gomorrah

Kevin Madison

ISBN: 978-1-7377003-9-5 paperback

ISBN: 978-1-7377003-2-6 ebook

Cover design and publishing assistance by The Happy Self-Publisher
Published by Madison Christian Books, LLC

Table of Contents

Introduction

Many have enquired about the United States of America's status during the biblical end times prophecy. Mainly, where does she fit within God's plan for the final seven years of human rule history on the earth as outlined in the biblical books of Daniel and Revelation. This biblical period is called by several names: The Day of the Lord, Jacob's Trouble, The Tribulation / Great Tribulation.

Is America mentioned by name?

What will be America's role?

Will America continue to be the sole "superpower" during the tribulation years?

If America is not mentioned, does this mean that she is no longer a nation, no longer a "superpower"? What happened to her?

Let us investigate the most likely faith of America, the Beautiful.

CHAPTER 1

THE CLARITY OF JUDGMENT

While most believe, as I did previously, that the only reason the Lord rained down fire and brimstone upon the cities of Sodom, Gomorrah and the cities of the plains surrounding them were because of homosexuality, it was significantly more than that, as most of the nations during those days had their bouts with sexual immorality as well. Nevertheless, the word of God unmistakably, unequivocally, and unapologetically declares that homosexuality is and will forever be, an abomination to the Lord.

"²² You shall not lie with a male as with a woman. It is an abomination." **Leviticus 18:22**

"¹³ If a man lies with a male as he lies with a woman, both of them have committed an abomination. They shall surely be put to death. Their blood shall be upon them." **Leviticus 20:13**

"²⁶ For this reason God gave them up to vile passions. For even their women exchanged the natural use for what is against nature. ²⁷ Likewise also the men, leaving the natural use of the woman, burned in their lust for one another, men with men committing what is shameful, and receiving in themselves the penalty of their error which was due." **Romans 1:26-27**

Therefore, let us not get into semantics concerning what is righteous and what is wicked in God's eyes. It does not matter what we think or believe. Only the word of God is established in the heavens and on the earth that it will never return unto Him void. As surely as God's words proceed out of His mouth, they will go forth and accomplish the things where unto He has sent them. According to the word of God there are degrees of sinful acts. Nevertheless, all sins are heinous in God's sight, and all sins will be punished if they remain unrepented of and upon the guilty person who committed them.

As mentioned, many times in the past, the best commentary on the Bible is the Bible. When we research all that the Bible has to say about Sodom and Gomorrah, we find the answers to the reasons the cities were judge so severely by the Lord. Let us not forget that the Lord is no respecter of persons, and his holiness never changes. Therefore, we must never believe that judgment like that placed upon Sodom and Gomorrah cannot happen today. The Lord, through His infinite wisdom, and mighty power, may choose to select a different method of destruction, yet the purpose of judgment remains the same. That purpose is to the praise of His glory, the justice of His righteousness, and the majesty of His holiness.

CHAPTER 2

The Comprehensibility of Judgment

The Incommunicable Attributes of God

An attribute of God is something true about Him. It is with great difficulty and infinite lack of understanding that we humans view the attributes of God. Even attempting to describe the Lord in mere words absolutely falls short of depicting who He is, as our vocabulary simply cannot ascertain the depths and heights to which God exists. Even we, as redeemed children, only see, hear, and know in part but there will soon come a day where we will behold the Lord face to face. I shudder at the thought.

[12] For now we see in a mirror, dimly, but then face to face. Now I know in part, but then I shall know just as I also am known. **1 Corinthians 13:12**

These attributes define the very person, nature, and character of the Most High God, who by mere definition, is undefinable except by that which He alone chooses to reveal concerning Himself unto His creation.

You may ask: "Why is that important?"

The Lord's attributes are important because they define the true nature of the unknowable God.

What do I mean by unknowable?

Well, I will allow the word of God to provide the answer to that question.

"⁹ Who does great things, and unsearchable, marvelous things without number." **Job 5:9**

"¹⁰ He does great things past finding out, yes, wonders without number." **Job 9:10**

"⁷ Can you search out the deep things of God? Can you find out the limits of the Almighty? ⁸ They are higher than heaven what can you do? Deeper than Sheol—what can you know? ⁹ Their measure is longer than the earth and broader than the sea." **Job 11:7-9**

"³ Great is the LORD, and greatly to be praised; and His greatness is unsearchable. **Psalms 145:3**

"³³ Oh, the depth of the riches both of the wisdom and knowledge of God! How unsearchable are His judgments and His ways past finding out! ³⁴ "For who has known the mind of the LORD? Or who has become His counselor?" ³⁵ "Or who has first given to Him and it shall be repaid to him?" ³⁶ For of Him and through Him and to Him are all things, to whom be glory forever. Amen." **Romans 11:33-36**

Let us take a closer look at what God has chosen to reveal about Himself.

The list could be exhaustive. However, we will endeavor to provide the fifteen most common attributes communicated throughout the word of God and Christendom today. These are listed in no particular order.

1. **God is infinite.** This means that God is self-existing and without origin. The fact is that God is self-existent, that there was never a time or moment when He was not present throughout eternity past and will continue through eternity future. This attribute of God is perhaps the most difficult for us to understand. How is it possible for anyone to be self-existent? I do not know, but listen to the declaration of God.

   [10] "You are My witnesses," says the LORD, "And My servant whom I have chosen, that you may know and believe Me, and understand that I am He. Before Me there was no God formed, nor shall there be after Me. [11] I, even I, am the LORD, and besides Me there is no savior. [12] I have declared and saved, I have proclaimed, and there was no foreign god among you; therefore, you are My witnesses," Says the LORD, "that I am God. [13] Indeed before the day was, I am He; And there is no one who can deliver out of My hand; I work, and who will reverse it?" **Isaiah 43:10-13**

   There is only one human who has walked this earth who has declared this to be true of himself. This man traveled throughout his country proving his identity by producing signs, wonders, and many miracles, so many in fact, that if all were recorded, the books written concerning him would have filled the entire world.

Who is this man?

It is Jesus Christ.

Jesus stated, "²⁶For as the Father has life in Himself, so He has granted the Son to have life in Himself, ²⁷ and has given Him authority to execute judgment also, because He is the Son of Man. ²⁸ Do not marvel at this; for the hour is coming in which all who are in the graves will hear His voice ²⁹ and come forth—those who have done good, to the resurrection of life, and those who have done evil, to the resurrection of condemnation. **John 5:26-29**

With that statement, Jesus claimed to be the self-existent One who alone has life in himself. Jesus claimed to be the One true God.

In our finite capacity, it is impossible for us to understand the infinite God who exists outside of time and space from everlasting to everlasting.

2. **God is immutable.** This means that He never changes. Not only does God never change, but it is also an impossibility for Him to change. The Lord never changes His mind. Everything about Him remains the same from everlasting to everlasting. Whatever God says will come to pass and there isn't a possibility that it will not happen exactly how and when He declared it to be. His words cannot fail. This is the source of infinite joy and peace to all those who place their trust in Jesus Christ. What this all means is that God is dependable. We can trust His word and have absolute confidence in all that He speaks without concern of Him ever revoking a promise. He purposes all things in Himself and for His glory. Therefore,

believers can be assured that the God who promised us eternal life, which is in the One who is immutable, will surely bring it to pass.

"⁸Jesus Christ is the same yesterday, today, and forever."
Hebrews 13:8

I will inquire of you; Is it possible to improve upon perfection? If the answer to that question is no, then you have the perfect description of the immutable God. Living in this fallen sin-filled world, we have never seen or experienced anything remotely close to perfection. Therefore, we do not have a clue what it looks like. However, the Lord can never, has never, and will never be contaminated by sin. He has and will always be set apart from all that is not eternally holy.

3. **God is self-sufficient**. This means that God has no needs. This clearly set all creation apart from the creator. All creation works within the governmental rules of the realm wherein they reside, and those rules cannot be altered or broken. On the other hand, God is not bound by any of these things, He sustains them.

"¹⁴ Indeed heaven and the highest heavens belong to the LORD your God, also the earth with all that is in it."
Deuteronomy 10:14

"Blessed are You, LORD God of Israel, our Father, forever and ever. ¹¹ Yours, O LORD, is the greatness, the power and the glory, the victory and the majesty; for all that is in heaven and in earth is Yours; Yours is the kingdom, O LORD, and You are exalted as head over all. ¹² Both riches and honor come from You, and You reign over all. In Your hand is power and might; in Your hand it is to make great and to give strength to all. [13] "Now therefore, our God, we thank You and praise Your glorious name. [14] But who am I, and who are my people, that we should be able to offer so willingly as this? For all things come from You, And of Your own we have given You." **1 Chronicles 29:10-14**

"[10] For every beast of the forest is Mine, and the cattle on a thousand hills. [11] I know all the birds of the mountains, and the wild beasts of the field are Mine. [12] "If I were hungry, I would not tell you; for the world is Mine, and all its fullness." **Psalms 50:10-12**

Because God is the Self-Sufficient One, we can go to Him with all our needs and cast our cares upon Him. We never have to worry or become despondent as His never-ending well of living water will never run dry.

What do you need today? Only Christ can fulfill it. Do you need love? Do you need comfort? Do you need peace? Do you need deliverance? Do you need forgiveness? Do you need hope? Do you need joy? Are you lonely, timid, ashamed, and afraid?

There is no one too bad that they cannot be delivered from or forgiven of sin and there is no one too good that they need not be delivered from or forgiven of sin. The Lord God has treated His Son, Jesus Christ, as if He has committed all your sins. Jesus took the full wrath of God upon the cross to allow God to offer you deliverance and forgiveness. To prove that Jesus' sacrifice upon the cross was sufficient to satisfy His eternal wrath upon sin, God raised Jesus from the dead.

Would you like to be forgiven? Then confess to God that you are a wretched sinner and cannot deliver yourself. Ask God to forgive you of your sins and place them upon Jesus. Confess to God that you believe that Jesus died in your place and that God raised Jesus from the grave. Ask Jesus to save you.

Remember, He works all things after the counsel of His own will for His own purpose and goodness, to the praise of His glory. Therefore, the answer and response may not fit our profile, but it will be perfect.

4. **God is omnipotent.** This means that He alone is all powerful. Omni means "all." Potent means "power." These together means that God has all power in the heavens and on the earth. God is the creator and sustainer of all His creation. All creation waits upon Him, and He opens His hands to give them their meat in due season. It is in Him that all things consist. If the Lord would release his grip upon creation, it would cease to exist. God is able and powerful enough to do anything He wills without exerting any effort on His part to accomplish it. This means that a mere thought or spoken word uttered from the mouth of the Almighty will come to pass at the exact time and place that the thought entered His mind, or the words departed His lips.

[7] "Can you fathom the mysteries of God? Can you probe the limits of the Almighty? [8] They are higher than the heavens above what can you do? They are deeper than the depths below what can you know? [9] Their measure is longer than the earth and wider than the sea. [10] If he comes along and confines you in prison and convenes a court, who can oppose him?" **Job 11:7-10**

4 "His wisdom is profound; his power is vast. Who has resisted him and come out unscathed? 5 He moves mountains without their knowing it and overturns them in his anger. 6 He shakes the earth from its place and makes its pillars tremble. 7 He speaks to the sun, and it does not shine; he seals off the light of the stars. 8 He alone stretches out the heavens and treads on the waves of the sea. 9 He is the Maker of the Bear and Orion, the Pleiades and the constellations of the south. 10 He performs wonders that cannot be fathomed, miracles that cannot be counted. 11 When he passes me, I cannot see him; when he goes by, I cannot perceive him. 12 If he snatches away, who can stop him? Who can say to him, 'What are you doing?'" **Job 9:4-12**

The Lord's might know no limits, as the scriptures attest by the numerous instances that describe God as the Almighty.

17 "Ah, Sovereign LORD, you have made the heavens and the earth by your great power and outstretched arm. Nothing is too hard for you. 18 You show love to thousands but bring the punishment for the parents' sins into the laps of their children after them. Great and mighty God, whose name is the LORD Almighty, 19 great are your purposes and mighty are your deeds. Your eyes are open to the ways of all mankind; you reward each person according to their conduct and as their deeds deserve." **Jeremiah 32:17-19**

Jesus, yet again, laid claim to this title reserved only of the one true God.

"18 And Jesus came and spoke unto them, saying, all power is given unto me in heaven and in earth." **Matthew 28:18**

⁸ "I am the Alpha and the Omega," says the Lord God, "who is, and who was, and who is to come, the Almighty." **Revelation 1:8**

"Although such power might seem frightful, remember that God is good. He can do anything according to His infinite ability, but will do only those things that are consistent with Himself. That's why He can't lie, tolerate sin, or save impenitent sinners." John MacArthur

⁹ "Remember the former things, those of long ago; I am God, and there is no other; I am God, and there is none like me. ¹⁰ I make known the end from the beginning, from ancient times, what is still to come. I say, 'My purpose will stand, and I will do all that I please.'" **Isaiah 46:4-10**

5. **God is omniscient.** This means that God is all-knowing. He knows all things at once.

⁵ "With whom will you compare me or count me equal? To whom will you liken me that we may be compared?" **Isaiah 46:5**

Not only does God know all things at once; He hears and knows even the thoughts of our hearts and minds too. How many billions of people are there living upon the earth—eight billion? How many angels are there in heaven? How many demons are there in the heavens, on the earth and under the earth? How many billions of people are there currently in heaven and in Hades?

The Lord knows every thought of us all and all the animals too. It is recorded concerning the Lord that He is the beginning of wisdom and knowledge. This attribute was also declared pertaining to Jesus.

"[10] The fear of the LORD is the beginning of wisdom; all who follow his precepts have good understanding. To him belongs eternal praise." **Psalms 111:10**

"[10]The fear of the LORD is the beginning of wisdom, and knowledge of the Holy One is understanding." **Proverbs 9:10**

"[2] My goal is that they may be encouraged in heart and united in love, so that they may have the full riches of complete understanding, in order that they may know the mystery of God, namely, Christ, [3] in whom are hidden all the treasures of wisdom and knowledge." **Colossians 2:2-3**

Since God is omniscient, we can trust that he knows everything we are going through today and everything we will go through tomorrow. Nothing catches the Lord by surprise. Every choice that we make and every possible choice we can make is fully known unto the Lord. Hence, He is able to work all things for good, for those who love Him and obey Him.

When we meditate on this truth, especially considering his other attributes of goodness and love, it makes it easier to trust him and for us to live in full assurance of faith and hope. With all we have going on in our lives, from the very serious to the silly and mundane, the Lord knows the beginning, middle, and ending.

Listen to David as he meditates upon the Lord.

[1] "You have searched me, LORD, and you know me. [2] You know when I sit and when I rise; you perceive my

thoughts from afar. ³ You discern my going out and my lying down; you are familiar with all my ways. ⁴ Before a word is on my tongue you, LORD, know it completely. ⁵ You hem me in behind and before, and you lay your hand upon me. ⁶ Such knowledge is too wonderful for me, too lofty for me to attain." **Psalms 139:1-6**

6. **God is omnipresent.** The Lord is always present, at all times. He is never asleep, nor does He slumber and is always attentive over His creation, working all things according to the counsel of His will.

³ He will not allow your foot to be moved; He who keeps you will not slumber. ⁴ Behold, He who keeps Israel shall neither slumber nor sleep. **Psalms 121:3-4**

David had some interesting things to say about this as he attempted to hide from the presence of the Lord.

⁷ "Where can I go from your Spirit? Where can I flee from your presence? ⁸ If I go up to the heavens, you are there; if I make my bed in the depths, you are there. ⁹ If I rise on the wings of the dawn, if I settle on the far side of the sea, ¹⁰ even there your hand will guide me, your right hand will hold me fast. ¹¹ If I say, "Surely the darkness will hide me and the light become night around me," ¹² even the darkness will not be dark to you; the night will shine like the day, for darkness is as light to you." **Psalms 139:7-12**

¹⁵ "My frame was not hidden from you when I was made in the secret place, when I was woven together in the depths of the earth. ¹⁶ Your eyes saw my unformed body; all the days ordained for me were written in your book before one of them came to be." **Psalms 139:15-16**

To be omnipresent is to be in all places, at all times. This is the only way prayers from everyone around the world can be heard at once. While it is tempting to have the understanding that God is "in a place" as we consider being in a place, that is not necessarily true. What is of utmost importance to understand is that God is a Spirit, and His being is altogether different from physical matter. He exists outside of time and space, meaning that there is no clock, height, width, or depth to God. The Lord resides within another dimension to which none of His creation can obtain neither is it accessible to or by the five senses. Even the angels cannot enter this dimension, as they only comprehend what the Lord reveals of himself. The scriptures clearly testify of this truth in both the Old and New Testaments.

[20] But He said, "You cannot see My face; for no man shall see Me, and live." **Exodus 33:20**

[18] No one has seen God at any time. The only begotten Son, who is in the bosom of the Father, He has declared Him. **John 1:18**

[46] Not that anyone has seen the Father, except He who is from God; He has seen the Father. **John 6:46**

[16] And without controversy great is the mystery of godliness: God was manifested in the flesh, justified in the Spirit, seen by angels, preached among the Gentiles, believed on in the world, received up in glory. **1 Timothy 3:16**

[14] that you keep this commandment without spot, blameless until our Lord Jesus Christ's appearing, [15] which He will manifest in His own time, He who is the blessed and

only Potentate, the King of kings and Lord of lords, [16] who alone has immortality, dwelling in unapproachable light, whom no man has seen or can see, to whom be honor and everlasting power. Amen. **1 Timothy 6:14-16**

Nevertheless, He is with us, the fullness of his presence is all around us. This should bring deep comfort to Christians who struggle with loneliness and deep sorrow. In a very real way, God is always near us, and for those who have entrusted their eternal salvation to God's Son, He is alive in them through the Holy Spirit. Because of His eternal presence, believers can be assured that God is aware of everything happening in our lives. Although we are encouraged to pray concerning all things, the Lord knows what we have need of before we utter a word because He is living out His glorious purpose and will in our lives.

You say, "This cannot be because I am really struggling. Why hasn't He delivered me?"

He has already delivered you. This is the one fallacy of false teaching that believers' lives will be comfortable and cozy after receiving God's grace. This is not taught in the word of God. As a matter of fact, the opposite is stated. Nonetheless, the Lord has and will continue to work all things for our good, in accordance with His own purpose and plan. That ultimate plan is to conform all believers into the very image of His Son.

What does this mean to you? Being "conformed into the image of God's Son, Jesus Christ?" Do you not understand the depth of that statement?

Jesus is God! He is seated on the throne of the Father with all power and authority given to Him in the heavens and in earth. Jesus dwells in a light that no man has seen, and no man can approach. The expressed brightness from the glory of His majesty outshines the sun in its full strength. Our Savior and God is a consuming fire. He is holy!

This metamorphosis will never and can never fully transpire while we, the children of God, are living in these fleshly unregenerated bodies that Paul called the body of death.

"[14] We know that the law is spiritual; but I am unspiritual, sold as a slave to sin. [15] I do not understand what I do. For what I want to do I do not do, but what I hate I do. [16] And if I do what I do not want to do, I agree that the law is good. [17] As it is, it is no longer I myself who do it, but it is sin living in me. [18] For I know that good itself does not dwell in me, that is, in my sinful nature. For I have the desire to do what is good, but I cannot carry it out. [19] For I do not do the good I want to do, but the evil I do not want to do—this I keep on doing. [20] Now if I do what I do not want to do, it is no longer I who do it, but it is sin living in me that does it. [21] So I find this law at work: Although I want to do good, evil is right there with me. [22] For in my inner being I delight in God's law; [23] but I see another law at work in me, waging war against the law of my mind and making me a prisoner of the law of sin at work within me. [24] *What a wretched man I am! Who will rescue me from this body that is subject to death?* [25] Thanks be to God, who delivers me through Jesus Christ our Lord! So then,

I myself in my mind am a slave to God's law, but in my sinful nature a slave to the law of sin." **Romans 7:14-25**

How and when will Paul and all believers be fully delivered from the body of death?

[50] Now this I say, brethren, that flesh and blood cannot inherit the kingdom of God; nor does corruption inherit incorruption. [51] Behold, I tell you a mystery: We shall not all sleep, but we shall all be changed— [52] in a moment, in the twinkling of an eye, at the last trumpet. For the trumpet will sound, and the dead will be raised incorruptible, and we shall be changed. [53] *For this corruptible must put on incorruption, and this mortal must put on immortality.* [54] *So when this corruptible has put on incorruption, and this mortal has put on immortality, then shall be brought to pass the saying that is written: "Death is swallowed up in victory." [55] "O Death, where is your sting? O Hades, where is your victory?"* [56] The sting of death is sin, and the strength of sin is the law. [57] But thanks be to God, who gives us the victory through our Lord Jesus Christ. [58] Therefore, my beloved brethren, be steadfast, immovable, always abounding in the work of the Lord, knowing that your labor is not in vain in the Lord. **1 Corinthians 15:50-58**

Too many believers have this unbiblical view of our walk with the Lord after justification. They totally intertwine the work of Christ, which is positional, and the saving faith works of the believer, which is provisional. One is assured and secured in heaven by Christ while the other is experienced through obedience and yielding to the Holy Spirit. Note that Paul states two truths. First, I know that good itself does not dwell in me, that is, in my sinful nature. Second, it is sin living in me that does it (disobey God's will and word). Do you realize that Paul said this after he was caught up to the third heaven and returned to the earth? There are only two people according to the Bible who have ever visited heaven and lived to talk about it. One was told not to reveal anything about his visit (Paul) while the other was told to write everything he was an eyewitness to except what the seven thunders uttered (John). No other human being has ever been transported to the third heaven, where the heavenly temple of God is located, then returned to earth. The one who recorded his visits wrote the book of Revelation. Paul was told never to discuss what he saw. Therefore, all these other accounts about heaven are absolutely false and from the devil.

This battle with our fleshly bodies and its wicked appetites will continue until the day Christ returns to rapture the church or we pass through the valley of the shadow of death. Either way, we should not be fearful as unbelievers who have no hope.

Why do unbelievers have no hope? Because everything that these earth dwellers live for will be taken from them in a single moment, at death. Then even that which they no longer have will also be taken away forever when they are judged and found guilty at the Great White Throne Judgment.

What will be taken away forever from the unbeliever? Hope of redemption.

True believers have hope and can never lose it. Unbelievers' desires hope but they do not possess it and never will obtain it.

Why can't believers lose their hope and unbelievers never obtain hope? Because believers' hope is a person, our Lord and God Jesus Christ.

"²⁰ We wait in hope for the LORD; he is our help and our shield. ²¹ In him our hearts rejoice, for we trust in his holy name. ²² May your unfailing love be with us, *LORD, even as we put our hope in you.*" **Psalms 33:20-22**

"²⁷ To them God has chosen to make known among the Gentiles the glorious riches of this mystery, *which is Christ in you, the hope of glory.*" **Colossians 1:27**

"¹¹ For the grace of God has appeared that offers salvation to all people. ¹² It teaches us to say "No" to ungodliness and worldly passions, and to live self-controlled, upright and godly lives in this present age, ¹³ *while we wait for the blessed hope—the appearing of the glory of our great God and Savior, Jesus Christ,* ¹⁴ who gave himself for us to redeem us from all wickedness and to purify for himself a people that are his very own, eager to do what is good." **Titus 2:11-14**

Our faith and hope are not in our abilities to be or do good. Neither is it for earthly health or possessions. It is for a Savior and a heavenly homecoming.

"³ Praise be to the God and Father of our Lord Jesus Christ! In his great mercy he has *given us new birth into a living hope through the resurrection of Jesus Christ from the dead,* ⁴ and into an inheritance that can never perish, spoil or fade. This inheritance is kept in heaven for you, ⁵ who through faith are shielded by God's power until the coming of the salvation that is ready to be revealed in the last time. ⁶ In all this you greatly rejoice, though now for a little while you may have had to suffer grief in all kinds of trials…²¹ Through him you believe in God, who raised him from the dead and glorified him, and *so your faith and hope are in God.*" **1 Peter 1:3-6, 21**

Stop listening to people who instruct you to focus on earthly possessions such as health, wealth, and earthly wisdom, which will all be consumed when the Lord dissolves by fire the current heavens and earth. These things are under the curse of Genesis 3. Do you understand why we get sick? Just look around you. Everything about us is dying. The entire universe is polluted. If not for the goodness and mercy of God, all creation would kill itself within a week, for certain seven years. That is a reference to Revelation and Matthew 24 where Jesus removes the restraining power of evil, the Holy Spirit, and allows the demons and mankind to perform their wickedness to its maximum capacities. You don't want to be here for that when 94% of the population dies in seven years.

"³ Above all, you must understand that in the last days scoffers will come, scoffing and following their own evil desires. ⁴ They will say, "Where is this 'coming' he promised? Ever since our ancestors died, everything goes on as it has since the beginning of creation." ⁵ But they deliberately forget that long ago by God's word the heavens came into being and the earth was formed out of water and by water. ⁶ By these waters also the world of that time was deluged and destroyed. *⁷ By the same word the present heavens and earth are reserved for fire, being kept for the day of judgment and destruction of the ungodly.* ¹⁰ But the day of the Lord will come like a thief. *The heavens will disappear with a roar; the elements will be destroyed by fire, and the earth and everything done in it will be laid bare.*" **2 Peter 3:3-7, 10**

We are strangers, foreigners, and pilgrims on this earth, journeying to the Father's house in which His Son has prepared for us a room in the heavenly Jerusalem.

"⁸ By faith Abraham, when called to go to a place he would later receive as his inheritance, obeyed and went, even though he did not know where he was going. ⁹ By faith he made his home in the promised land like a stranger in a foreign country; he lived in tents, as did Isaac and Jacob, who were heirs with him of the same promise. ¹⁰ For he was looking forward to the city with foundations, whose architect and builder is God." **Hebrews 11:8-10**

"¹¹ Dear friends, I urge you, as foreigners and exiles, to abstain from sinful desires, which wage war against your soul. ¹² Live such good lives among the pagans that, though they accuse you of doing wrong, they may see your good deeds and glorify God on the day he visits us." **1 Peter 2:11-12**

CHAPTER 3

THE COHERENCE OF JUDGMENT

The Communicable Attributes of God

We continue to define God's attributes as they correlate with His judgments, seeking to understand what types of questions we are attempting to answer. Questions such as: Who is God? What is God like? What kind of God is He? While fully comprehending the infinite God is impossible for us to fully comprehend as finite creators, God does make Himself known in various ways. This self-revelation is all made possible through His Word and in creation. Through these avenues, we can moderately begin to coherently comprehend our awesome Creator and God.

God is unlike anything or anyone we could ever know or imagine. He is one of a kind, unique and without comparison.

You may ask: "How is that possible?"

I will attempt to make this clear with a simple yet irrefutable example. What do we see every day that God has never seen?

Our equal.

Listen to the Almighty. [10] "You are My witnesses," says the LORD, "And My servant whom I have chosen, that you may know and believe Me, and understand that I am He. *Before Me there was no God formed, nor shall there be after Me.* [11] I, even I, am the LORD, and *besides Me there is no savior.* [12] I have declared and saved, I have proclaimed, and there was no foreign god among you; Therefore, you are My witnesses," Says the LORD, "that I am God. [13] Indeed before the day was, I am He; And there is no one who can deliver out of My hand; I work, and who will reverse it?" **Isaiah 43:10-13**

So, what do I mean by communicable attributes? Essentially, they are qualities that both God and humans possess, though only He possesses them perfectly. There is coming a day, beloved, that every true believer in Christ longs for—total and complete victory over our flesh, the world, death, hell, and the grave.

[50] Now this I say, brethren, that flesh and blood cannot inherit the kingdom of God; nor does corruption inherit incorruption. [51] Behold, I tell you a mystery: We shall not all sleep, but we shall all be changed [52] in a moment, in the twinkling of an eye, at the last trumpet. For the trumpet will sound, and the dead will be raised incorruptible, and we shall be changed. [53] For this corruptible must put on incorruption, and this mortal must put on immortality. [54] So when this corruptible has put on incorruption, and this mortal has put on immortality, then shall be brought to pass the saying that is written: "Death is swallowed up in victory." [55] "O Death, where is your sting? O Grave, where is your victory?" [56] The sting of death is sin, and the strength of sin is the law. [57] But thanks be to God, who gives us the victory through our Lord Jesus Christ. [58] Therefore, my beloved brethren, be steadfast, immovable, always abounding in the work of the Lord, knowing that your labor is not in vain in the Lord. **1 Corinthians 15:50-58**

Though we know in part today and see through the stained glass, there is soon coming a day when all the saints of God will shout, sing, and rejoice before the throne of His holiness. In that day, every prayer will be answered immediately and directly because we will know His perfect will.

¹ Behold what manner of love the Father has bestowed on us, that we should be called children of God! Therefore, the world does not know us, because it did not know Him. ² Beloved, now we are children of God; and it has not yet been revealed what we shall be, but we know that when He is revealed, we shall be like Him, for we shall see Him as He is. **1 John 3:1-2**

We shall behold Him in all His wisdom, faithfulness, goodness, justice, mercy, grace, love, glory, and holiness.

7. **God is wise.** The wisdom of God is perfect. This attribute is different than God knowing all things. In knowing all things, God's ability to perfectly create and bring His will to fruition brings to light supreme wisdom of the Most High God.

    After revealing God's plan for Israel and the Church in Romans 9, 10, and 11, Paul becomes overwhelmed with joy and praise at how these things are worked out in the plan of the Lord. In his exuberance, Paul let's out a doxology declaring, "Oh, the depth of the riches both of the wisdom and knowledge of God! How unsearchable are his judgments, and his ways past finding out! "For who has known the mind of the LORD? Or who has become His counselor?" "Or who has first given to Him and it shall be repaid to him?" For of Him and through Him and to Him are all things, to whom be glory forever. Amen." **Romans 11:33-36**

Wisdom is more than head knowledge and intelligence. A truly wise person is someone who understands most of all there is to know about a certain subject, which will enable them to make the best decision. All that person's being will be aligned with the decision, rendering failure nearly impossible. Nevertheless, even the wisest person who has ever walked the earth, Adam, the first man God created, cannot come remotely close to the wisdom of God, as there is nothing, He does not know about anything.

While it is possible for humans to grow in wisdom, that is not a possibility with God. He is infinitely wise, and all wisdom is stored within Himself.

Oh Lord, I stand in awe of You. For you, my God, give wisdom. From Your mouth come knowledge and understanding. You store up sound wisdom for the upright in heart and are a shield to those who walk uprightly. It is by wisdom that You founded the earth, by understanding You established the heavens, and by Your knowledge the depths were broken up and clouds dropped down the rain and the dew. Who is like You, O Lord? Who can call those things that be not as though they are? For there is no other God aside from You. All hail the great King, the Lord of hosts is His name.

[10] The fear of the LORD is the beginning of wisdom; a good understanding have all those who do His commandments. His praise endures forever. **Psalms 111:10**

8. **God is faithful.** As the self-existing One, the Lord is infinitely and unchangingly true. Not only can He not

fail but it can never ever become a possibility that He can fail. God's faithfulness is linked to His eternally holy nature, meaning that He must always be true to Himself.

Listen to Moses' declaration concerning the Most High, [9] "Therefore know that the LORD your God, He is God, the faithful God who keeps covenant and mercy for a thousand generations with those who love Him and keep His commandments;" **Deuteronomy 7:9**

"[9] God is faithful, by whom you were called into the fellowship of His Son, Jesus Christ our Lord." **1 Corinthians 1:9**

"[13] No temptation has overtaken you except such as is common to man; but God is faithful, who will not allow you to be tempted beyond what you are able, but with the temptation will also make the way of escape, that you may be able to bear it." **1 Corinthians 10:13**

This alone should make those who have placed their trust in Jesus for salvation based solely on His word, rejoice beyond all measure. We can be certain without the fear of God's failure or happenstance that His word will fail. The security found in God's faithfulness is beyond anything man has ever experienced in this world since there is nothing created that cannot ultimately be destroyed. However, we serve an infinite God who upholds all things by the word of His power, who has declared all those who have placed their trust in the death, burial and resurrection of His Son, Christ Jesus the Lord, righteous in His sight.

¹ But now, thus says the LORD, who created you, O Jacob, and He who formed you, O Israel: "Fear not, for I have redeemed you; I have called you by your name; You are Mine. ² When you pass through the waters, I will be with you; and through the rivers, they shall not overflow you. When you walk through the fire, you shall not be burned, Nor shall the flame scorch you. **Isaiah 43:1-2**

Even though it is unfathomable to us because we have never experienced anything like the faithfulness of God due to the introduction of sin into the world, we can look to the Holy One and His divine character to be certain of His plans and goodness. All that He has spoken, He shall surely bring it to pass.

²³ Now may the God of peace Himself sanctify you completely; and may your whole spirit, soul, and body be preserved blameless at the coming of our Lord Jesus Christ. ²⁴ **He who calls you is faithful, who also will do it. 1 Thessalonians 5:23-24**

9. **God is good.** The Lord is infinitely unchangingly full of goodness and kindness. How do we know this? We witness it every single day. No matter how sinful mankind has become, God continues to pour out goodness and kindness upon us. The sun rises and sets, the moon controls the tides, the stars give their light, the rain falls upon the just and the unjust, the trees supply their fruit, and we are all fed daily. Do not attempt to convince me that God is not good when He does not strike us dead when we rebel against His holiness daily.

Some of us would has taken out quite a few people if we were endowed with God's power—some for just driving too slow or too fast. We are so fickle. Nevertheless, that is not how the Lord conducts His business. We must understand that with all power comes eternal restraint and longsuffering. Yet, one day this great restraint will end and the dam of God's goodness holding back the ocean of God's wrath will break. In that day, I would not want to be on the dry side of the dam.

How can we know with absolute certainty that God is good?

Will you just stop for a few minutes? No, I mean stop everything. Clear your mind. Now, think about all the times you could have and should have been injured or dead. Life is not easy, and we all bare our own burdens. Yet, the goodness of God never fails to deliver us from death today. Though tomorrow is not promised, we behold God's goodness today. This is the form of goodness that the Lord declares should lead us to repentance. It reveals the true nature of the Most High God, that He would rather have mercy than to judge guilt and pour out His wrath.

[4] Or do you despise the riches of His goodness, forbearance, and longsuffering, **not knowing that the goodness of God leads you to repentance? Romans 2:4**

Listen to how good God is:

"[8] Good and upright is the LORD; Therefore, He teaches sinners in the way." **Psalms 25:8**

"⁸ Oh, taste and see that the LORD is good; Blessed is the man who trusts in Him!" **Psalms 34:8**

"⁵ For You, Lord, are good, and ready to forgive, and abundant in mercy to all those who call upon You." **Psalms 86:5**

"⁵ For the LORD is good; His mercy is everlasting, And His truth endures to all generations." **Psalms 100:5**

"¹ Oh, give thanks to the LORD, for He is good! For His mercy endures forever." **Psalms 107:1**

Oh, my friend, the Lord is a good God. You and I are a living testimony of His goodness. If He is this good to you while you are His enemy, how do you think He will treat you if you become one of His children? Will you trust Him today by confessing your sinfulness, repenting of your sinfulness, and trusting in Jesus' death, burial, and resurrection for salvation? The good God has called out to you and is waiting for your response.

10. **God is Just.** The Lord is infinitely unchangeably righteous and perfect in all He does. Not only is He perfectly righteous and just, but it is also impossible for Him not to be. Just is not what God does. Just is who God is. Justice is as much a part of the Lord's character as goodness, omnipotence, or omnipresence. God's justice is based upon His righteous standings, meaning that it originates from His perfection. Since He knows all things, including the secret motives behind everything we say and do, it is impossible for anyone to con God into believing something that is not true.

³ The eyes of the LORD are in every place, keeping watch on the evil and the good. **Proverbs 15:3**

The Lord must be true to Himself, as He cannot bypass sin, nor can He unambiguously pardon the sinner. They are one and the same in the eyes of a just God. Since the sin and sinner cannot be separated, it leaves the Lord with no choice but to charge the sinner guilty on all counts of wickedness and coming short of His glorious standards. Convicted, the sinner must now suffer forever and ever the eternal wrath of the just God.

Who are these sinners?

We are, all of us! The word of God declares that every person born into this world are sinners by nature. This means, that sin is genetic. It is passed down from fathers and mothers to the child. Sin makes us all unclean. Listen to Job, David, and Paul.

⁴how can he be pure who is born of a woman? **Job 25:4b**

⁵ Behold, I was brought forth in iniquity, and in sin my mother conceived me. **Psalms 51:5**

⁴ Who can bring a clean thing out of an unclean? No one! **Job 14:4**

¹⁴ "What is man, that he could be pure? And he who is born of a woman, that he could be righteous? ¹⁵ If God puts no trust in His saints, and the heavens are not pure in His sight, ¹⁶ How much less man, who is abominable and filthy, who drinks iniquity like water. **Job 15:14-16**

[12] Therefore, just as sin came into the world through one man, and death through sin, and so death spread to all men because all sinned. **Romans 5:12**

"The Rock! His work is perfect, for all His ways are just; A God of faithfulness and without injustice, Righteous and upright is He." **Deuteronomy 32:4**

The better question is: "How can a just God justify the unjust sinner?" The Bible makes it clear that this is an impossibility, for it is impossible for the unjust person to perform any act that can measure up to the absolute holiness of God. Furthermore, the Holy One of Israel requires a blood sacrifice to satisfy His wrath upon sin and the sinner. This means that the soul that sins must die.

How then can a dead person offer up themselves? It is not possible and even if it were possible, all men are considered unjust sinners. Hence, we are all unclean. The justice of God will not allow Him to accept an unclean unholy sacrifice.

Then how can a just God justify the unjust? By becoming a man and sacrificing Himself.

Read this verse very carefully.

"[17] Therefore, if anyone is in Christ, he is a new creation; old things have passed away; behold, all things have become new. [18] Now all things are of God, who has reconciled us to Himself through Jesus Christ, and has given us the ministry of reconciliation, [19] that is, that **God was in Christ reconciling the world to Himself**, not imputing their trespasses to them, and has committed to us the word of reconciliation." **2 Corinthians 5:17-19**

This verse clearly states that the God of all creation inserted Himself into the body of the man named Jesus Christ thereby making the man Jesus the Son of God and God himself. Jesus Christ was, is, and shall forever be the One true God. Therefore, God cannot just overlook or bypass our sins. God sacrificed Himself and raised that body from the dead to allow us to have forgiveness from our sins and obsolescence from the punishment of those sins.

Paul declared this truth to the elders in the church at Ephesus.

"^{27} For I have not hesitated to proclaim to you the whole will of God. ^{28} Keep watch over yourselves and all the flock of which the Holy Spirit has made you overseers. Be shepherds of the church of God, which He bought with His own blood." **Acts 20:27-28**

God is a spirit; from where did He get blood? From the man, Jesus Christ. Do you now understand that there is no bypassing the cross and the resurrection of Jesus? Without the cross of Jesus Christ, we all must face the justice and wrath of a holy God and are all doomed to hell, but thank the heavenly Father for His sacrificial lamb, Jesus Christ!

Everyone deserves justice from the Just God. Nevertheless, the Lord God in His great mercy, kindness, and longsuffering has made available through the death, burial, and resurrection of His son, Jesus Christ, access to receive mercy and a home in heaven. Some will accept God's offer to repent, believe, and obey. All others will receive justice and be cast into hell, the lake of fire, forever.

"Through the work of Christ in atonement, justice is not violated but satisfied when God spares a sinner." AW Tozer

Oh my Lord, how can it be? That you, my God, would die for me! For what can wash away my sins? Nothing but the blood of Jesus. For what can make me whole again? Nothing but the blood of Jesus. Oh, precious is the flow, that makes me white as snow, no other fount I know, nothing but the blood of Jesus.

For there is a fountain filled with blood drawn from Emanuel's veins, where sinners plunge beneath this flood, lose all their guilt and stains. Oh, the precious blood of Jesus, it will never lose its power.

[18] "Come now, and let us reason together," Says the LORD, "Though your sins are like scarlet, they shall be as white as snow; Though they are red like crimson, they shall be as wool. **Isaiah 1:18**

The Father is calling you right now. Will you come and wash away your sins?

[6] When Jesus saw him lying there, and knew that he already had been in that condition a long time, He said to him, **"Do you want to be made well?" John 5:6**

Well, do you?

11. **God is merciful.** This means that the Lord is infinitely compassionate and forbearing. Because He is infinitely merciful, God cannot hold resentments. He acts upon His judgments then after they are satisfied, He is free to show mercy. The marvelous thing about the Lord's character is that He can administer both at the same time. Remember, the Lord exists outside of time and space. Therefore, everything that He does is being done at this moment in time. There is no tomorrow with Him, as time was created for man as a reference and not for God. He holds all these things in His hand.

So, how does God administer mercy? On what basis is His mercy released?

"⁵...For I, the LORD your God, am a jealous God, visiting the iniquity of the fathers upon the children to the third and fourth generations of those who hate Me, ⁶ but **showing mercy to thousands, to those who love Me and keep My commandments.**" Exodus 20:5-6

"⁵ Now the LORD descended in the cloud and stood with him there and proclaimed the name of the LORD. ⁶ And the LORD passed before him and proclaimed, "The LORD, the LORD God, **merciful** and gracious, longsuffering, and abounding in goodness and truth, ⁷ **keeping mercy for thousands, forgiving iniquity and transgression and sin,** by no means clearing the guilty, visiting the iniquity of the fathers upon the children and the children's children to the third and the fourth generation.""" **Exodus 34:5-7**

"⁹ Therefore know that the LORD your God, He is God, the faithful God who keeps covenant and **mercy for a thousand generations with those who love Him and keep His commandments;** ¹⁰ and He repays those who hate Him to their face, to destroy them. He will not be slack with him who hates Him; He will repay him to his face." **Deuteronomy 7:9-10**

"¹⁵ For He says to Moses, "I will have mercy on whomever I will have mercy, and I will have compassion on whomever I will have compassion." ¹⁶ So then it is not of him who wills, nor of him who runs, but of God who shows mercy." **Romans 9:15-16**

The Lord God upon His own volition and sovereign authority determines who will be the recipient of His mercy. There is nothing an individual, group, or people can do that would make God look down on them from heaven and say, "Wow, what nice people they are. They have earned my mercy today."

Paul summed it up this way in **Romans 9:18**, "¹⁸ Therefore He has mercy on whom He wills, and whom He wills He hardens."

Paul adds.

"¹⁹ One of you will say to me: "Then why does God still blame us? For who is able to resist his will?"" **Romans 9:19**

Then Paul finished the argument with this declaration.

"²⁰ But who are you, a human being, to talk back to God? "Shall what is formed say to the one who formed it, 'Why did you make me like this?'" ²¹ Does not the potter have the right to make out of the same lump of clay some pottery for special purposes and some for common use?" Romans 9:20-21

My friend, what needs to be understood is this.

"[14]...that you keep this commandment without spot, blameless until our Lord Jesus Christ's appearing, [15] which He will manifest in His own time, He **who is the blessed and only Potentate,** the King of kings and Lord of lords, [16] who alone has immortality, dwelling in unapproachable light, whom no man has seen or can see, to whom be honor and everlasting power. Amen." 1 Timothy 6:14-16

God is a Monarch, a Dictator. He rules alone, without counsel and without administrative assistance. He rules and fills all in all and upholds it all by the word of His power. When we hear descriptions like monarch and dictator, it carries with it the stigma of authoritative overlord that cares about nothing but himself and family. What God presents is what He has written. When the godly rule, the people rejoice. When the wicked rule, the people mourn. The Lord's very essence is godly and there is none like Him. Therefore, to be ruled by the King of Glory is to live in a world wherein righteousness, peace, goodness, and kindness reigns.

You say, what will that world look like?

I will let the Lord himself describe it for you.

[1] Then a shoot will spring from the stem of Jesse, and a branch from his roots will bear fruit. [2] The Spirit of the LORD will rest on Him, the spirit of wisdom and understanding, The spirit of counsel and strength, the spirit of knowledge

and the fear of the LORD. ³ And He will delight in the fear of the LORD, and He will not judge by what His eyes see, Nor make a decision by what His ears hear; ⁴ But with righteousness He will judge the poor and decide with fairness for the afflicted of the earth; and He will strike the earth with the rod of His mouth, and with the breath of His lips He will slay the wicked. ⁵ Also righteousness will be the belt about His loins, and faithfulness the belt about His waist. ⁶ And the wolf will dwell with the lamb, and the leopard will lie down with the young goat, and the calf and the young lion and the fatling together; and a little boy will lead them. ⁷ Also the cow and the bear will graze, their young will lie down together, and the lion will eat straw like the ox. ⁸ The nursing child will play by the hole of the cobra, and the weaned child will put his hand on the viper's den. ⁹ They will not hurt or destroy in all My holy mountain, for the earth will be full of the knowledge of the LORD as the waters cover the sea. ¹⁰ Then in that day the nations will resort to the root of Jesse, Who will stand as a signal for the peoples; and His resting place will be glorious. **Isaiah 11:1-10**

What a glorious time we will have with the LORD during the millennium and eternal ages!

12. **God is gracious.** This means that He is always kind, gentle, and pleasant. "As mercy is God's goodness confronting human misery and guilt," AW Tozer writes, "so grace is His goodness directed toward human debt and demerit. It is by his grace that God imputes merit where none previously existed and declares no debt to be where one had been before."

Who has done anything for the Lord that he was not first equipped by the Lord to accomplish? Mankind has absolutely no ability to merit anything from God as man is totally corrupt from nature and cannot appear in the presence of God without a mediator.

"[21] But now apart from the law the righteousness of God has been made known, to which the Law and the Prophets testify. [22] This righteousness is given through faith in Jesus Christ to all who believe. There is no difference between Jew and Gentile, [23] for all have sinned and fall short of the glory of God, [24] and all are justified freely by his grace through the redemption that came by Christ Jesus. [25] God presented Christ as a sacrifice of atonement, through the shedding of his blood to be received by faith. He did this to demonstrate his righteousness, because in his forbearance he had left the sins committed beforehand unpunished [26] he did it to demonstrate his righteousness at the present time, so as to be just and the one who justifies those who have faith in Jesus." **Romans 3:21-26**

It is by this marvelous grace that salvation is distributed by the Holy Spirit unto the ungodly.

"[6] You see, at just the right time, when we were still powerless, Christ died for the ungodly. [7] Very rarely will anyone die for a righteous person, though for a good person someone might possibly dare to die. [8] But God demonstrates his own love for us in this: While we were still sinners, Christ died for us." **Romans 5:6-8**

Why would God extend grace only to the ungodly and not the godly too? Because there are no godly people, for it is written that all have sinned and come short of the glory of God as we stated in **Romans 3:23.**

Yet, God's grace is not just unmerited favor that allows the Spirit of God to transfer the ungodly sinner from the kingdom of the devil into the kingdom of God. On the contrary, God's grace teaches the new convert how to live. You see, saving faith produces a living hope, whereby grace is the entrance way and Jesus, himself, is the door.

God's grace isn't an act bestowed upon a believer; grace is part of God's character. It is impossible to separate grace at any time from the King of Glory, the Lord of hosts.

[11] For the grace of God has appeared, bringing salvation for all people, [12] training us to renounce ungodliness and worldly passions, and to live self-controlled, upright, and godly lives in the present age, [13] waiting for our blessed hope, the appearing of the glory of our great God and Savior Jesus Christ, [14] who gave himself for us to redeem us from all lawlessness and to purify for himself a people for his own possession who are zealous for good works. **Titus 2:11-14**

This is such good news that we are commanded to share it with every tribe, nation, people, and tongue. This grace is made available to all, and all are in need of God's grace.

13. **God is loving.** "[7] Beloved, let us love one another, for love is of God; and everyone who loves is born of God and knows God. [8] He who does not love does not know God, **for God is love.**" **1 John 4:7-8**

No one can declare this truth more clearly than the Lord himself. Note that the Spirit of God states that God is love and not that He have love. Love is manifested, revealed, and realized in the very person and nature of the one true God. All that He is and all that He does originates from the depths of His being, which is defined as love.

One could state that one of the primary purposes for creation is to allow others to experience His love. This is the same love that the triune God has for each other, Father, Son, and the Holy Spirit. This is an eternal love that cannot by its very nature, originating in the eternal God, ever come to an end. This is the reason Paul could boldly proclaim to the Roman believers concerning God's love for His children.

"[31] What then shall we say to these things? If God is for us, who can be against us? [32] He who did not spare His own Son, but delivered Him up for us all, how shall He not with Him also freely give us all things? [33] Who shall bring a charge against God's elect? It is God who justifies. [34] Who is he who condemns? It is Christ who died, and furthermore is also risen, who is even at the right hand of God, who also makes intercession for us. [35]Who shall separate us from the love of Christ? Shall tribulation, or distress, or persecution, or famine, or nakedness, or peril, or sword? [36] As it is written: "For Your sake we are killed all day long; We are accounted as sheep for the slaughter." [37] Yet in all these things we are more than conquerors through Him who loved us. [38] For I am persuaded that neither death nor life, nor angels nor principalities nor powers, nor things present nor things to come, [39] nor height nor depth, nor any other created thing, shall be able to separate us from the love of God which is in Christ Jesus our Lord." **Romans 8:31-39**

What is behind this bold proclamation? There are two primary reasons:

1. The Lord of His own volition decided to love us, yet we must understand that this love is not found in us but in His Son.

   "[9] In this the love of God was manifested toward us, that God has sent His only begotten Son into the world, that we might live through Him. [10] In this is love, not that we loved God, but that He loved us and sent His Son to be the propitiation for our sins." **1 John 4:9-10**

2. It is because the believer has the Spirit of Christ, who is love, living inside of Him.

   [5] Now hope does not disappoint, because the love of God has been poured out in our hearts by the Holy Spirit who was given to us. **Romans 5:5**

   [8] But God demonstrates His own love toward us, in that while we were still sinners, Christ died for us. **Romans 5:8**

   "[13] In Him you also trusted, after you heard the word of truth, the gospel of your salvation; in whom also, having believed, **you were sealed with the Holy Spirit of promise**, [14] **who is the guarantee of our inheritance** until the redemption of the

purchased possession, to the praise of His glory."
Ephesians 1:13-14

Once the Spirit of Love takes up residence within us, we too become partakers and exhibits of the manifested love of our heavenly Father. This is described beautifully by the Apostle Peter.

[3] His divine power has granted to us all things that pertain to life and godliness, through the knowledge of him who called us to his own glory and excellence, [4] by which he has granted to us his precious and very great promises, **so that through them you may become partakers of the divine nature**, having escaped from the corruption that is in the world because of sinful desire. **2 Peter 1:3-4**

You may ask: "What are the types of exhibits?"

The Lord Jesus gave us the most important exhibits.

[37] Jesus said to him, "**'You shall love the LORD your God with all your heart, with all your soul, and with all your mind.'** [38] This is the first and great commandment. [39] And the second is like it: **You shall love your neighbor as yourself.'** [40] On these two commandments hang all the Law and the Prophets." **Matthew 22:37-40**

John provides the other two types of exhibits in 1 John 3. The Spirit of God has given us command to exhibit on this basis.

1. **The imperative of Love**, meaning that love for other believers, is not optional or an act. It is a genuine characteristic found within the newly created spirit

the Lord created within every believer upon baptizing into the body of Christ by the Holy Spirit.

a. [10] In this the children of God and the children of the devil are manifest: **Whoever does not practice righteousness is not of God, nor is he who does not love his brother.** [11] For this is the message that you heard from the beginning, that we should love one another, [12] not as Cain who was of the wicked one and murdered his brother. And why did he murder him? Because his works were evil and his brother's righteous. [13] Do not marvel, my brethren, if the world hates you. [14] **We know that we have passed from death to life, because we love the brethren.** He who does not love his brother abides in death. [15] Whoever hates his brother is a murderer, and you know that no murderer has eternal life abiding in him. **1 John 3:10-15**

2. **The outworking of Love**, meaning the tangible and visible works of saving faith.

a. [16] By this we know love, because He laid down His life for us. **And we also ought to lay down our lives for the brethren.** [17] **But whoever has this world's goods, and sees his brother in need, and shuts up his heart from him**, how does the love of God abide in him? [18] **My little children, let us not love in word or in tongue, but in deed and in truth.** [19] And by this we know that we are of the truth, and shall assure

our hearts before Him. [20] For if our heart condemns us, God is greater than our heart, and
knows all things. [21] Beloved, if our heart does
not condemn us, we have confidence toward
God. [22] And whatever we ask we receive from
Him, because we keep His commandments and
do those things that are pleasing in His sight. [23]
And this is His commandment: that we should
believe on the name of His Son Jesus Christ and
love one another, as He gave us commandment.
1 John 3:16-23

Do you see the difference? One is solely through the work
of Christ and the other is the work of the Holy Spirit
through our yielded obedience. Christ's work is singular,
performed only by Jesus accepted by the Father, while our
works of righteousness are plural, performed by the Spirit
of God, rewarded by Jesus at the judgment seat of Christ.
One is for salvation, which is our ticket into heaven, the
inner white garment declaring we have been made righteous, and entrance into the very presence of the thrice
Holy God.

[1] For we know that if our earthly house, this tent, is
destroyed, we have a building from God, a house not
made with hands, eternal in the heavens. [2] For in this we
groan, earnestly desiring to be clothed with our habitation
which is from heaven, [3] if indeed, having been clothed, we
shall not be found naked. **2 Corinthians 5:1-3**

[11] Then a white robe was given to each of them; and
it was said to them that they should rest a little while

longer, until both the number of their fellow servants and their brethren, who would be killed as they were, was completed. **Revelation 6:11**

[23] and be renewed in the spirit of your mind, [24] and that you put on the new man which was created according to God, in true righteousness and holiness. **Ephesians 4:23-24**

The other is our outer garment, which will be diverse in length based on our individual faith works and the heavenly authority awarded us in the kingdom of God forever. We see the Lord and His presence while here on earth through this manifested love. These two characteristics are evident.

1. **Seeing God through Love.** This is how we approach our heavenly Father and are familiar with His ways.

    a. [12] No one has seen God at any time. If we love one another, God abides in us, and His love has been perfected in us. **[13] By this we know that we abide in Him, and He in us, because He has given us of His Spirit.** [14] And we have seen and testify that the Father sent the Son as Savior of the world. [15] Whoever confesses that Jesus is the Son of God, God abides in him, and he in God. [16] And we have known and believed the love that God has for us. **God is love, and he who abides in love abides in God, and God in him. 1 John 4:12-16**

2. **The Consummation of Love.** How does it all come together, to please God and in revelation to the world?

   a. [17] This is how love is made complete among us so that **we will have confidence on the day of judgment**: In this world **we are like Jesus**. [18] There is **no fear** in love. But perfect love drives out fear, because fear has to do with punishment. The one who fears is not made perfect in love. [19] We love because he first loved us. **1 John 4:17-19**

3. **The walk of Love.** This is where the rubber meets the road, where our feet hit the pavement, where the rain waters the grass, where... anyhow, you know what I mean.

   a. [20] Whoever claims to love God yet hates a brother or sister is a liar. For whoever does not love their brother and sister, whom they have seen, cannot love God, whom they have not seen. [21] And he has given us this command: Anyone who loves God must also love their brother and sister. [1] Everyone who believes that Jesus is the Christ is born of God, and everyone who loves the Father loves his child as well. [2] This is how we know that we love the children of God: by loving God and carrying out his commands. [3] **In fact, this is love for God: to keep his commands. And his commands are not burdensome,** [4] for everyone born of God overcomes the world. This is the victory that has overcome the world, even our faith. [5] Who is it that overcomes the world? Only the one who believes that Jesus is the Son of God. **1 John 4:20-21, 5:1-5**

Isn't this wonderful beloved? We can live with full assurance that we are God's children, are loved of God and love Him. Loving God equates to willingly obeying God and traveling in the opposite direction of the ungodly world.

14. **God is Glorious.** [11] Who among the gods is like you, LORD? Who is like you, majestic in holiness, awesome in glory, working wonders? **Exodus 15:11**

What is meant by the glory of the Lord? It means that in and of Himself the Lord's radiant purity and beauty is a blinding light and a consuming fire. The word of God, at times exchanges the words brightness, fire, and majesty for glory, which perfectly describes the manifestation of the appearance of the Lord.

[3] God came from Teman, The Holy One from Mount Paran. Selah His glory covered the heavens, and the earth was full of His praise. [4] **His brightness was like the light; he had rays flashing from His hand**, and there His power was hidden. [5] Before Him went pestilence, and fever followed at His feet. **Habakkuk 3:3-5**

There are several examples of this in the word of God, as witnessed by those who have seen the Lord Jesus before and after His earthly tour. Listen to how Moses described the glory of the Lord as seen by the children of Israel at Mount Sinai.

¹⁵ When Moses went up on the mountain, the cloud covered it, ¹⁶ and the glory of the LORD settled on Mount Sinai. For six days the cloud covered the mountain, and on the seventh day the LORD called to Moses from within the cloud. ¹⁷ **To the Israelites the glory of the LORD looked like a consuming fire on top of the mountain.** Exodus 24:15-17

How did the children of Israel respond to the appearance of the glory of the Lord?

¹⁶ On the morning of the third day there was thunder and lightning, with a thick cloud over the mountain, and a very loud trumpet blast. **Everyone in the camp trembled.** ¹⁷ Then Moses led the people out of the camp to meet with God, and they stood at the foot of the mountain. ¹⁸ **Mount Sinai was covered with smoke, because the LORD descended on it in fire. The smoke billowed up from it like smoke from a furnace, and the whole mountain trembled violently.** ¹⁹ As the sound of the trumpet grew louder and louder, Moses spoke and the voice of God answered him. **Exodus 19:16-19**

How are we to respond to the very presence of God that resides within us today?

²⁸ Therefore, since we are receiving a kingdom that cannot be shaken, **let us be thankful, and so worship God acceptably with reverence and awe,** ²⁹ **for our "God is a consuming fire." Hebrews 12:28-29**

How do God's enemies respond to the presence of the God of all creation?

¹ The LORD reigns; let the earth rejoice; let the multitude of isles be glad! ² Clouds and darkness surround Him; righteousness and justice are the foundation of His throne. ³ **A fire goes before Him and burns up His enemies round about. Psalms 97:1-3**

His enemies are all consumed by the glory of His presence. This is how the Lord will destroy Satan and the anti-Christ.

⁷ Behold, **He is coming with clouds (the shekinah glory),** and every eye will see Him, even they who pierced Him. And all the tribes of the earth will mourn because of Him. Even so, Amen. **Revelation 1:7**

⁵ Do you not remember that when I was still with you, I told you these things? ⁶ And now you know what is restraining, that he may be revealed in his own time. ⁷ For the mystery of lawlessness is already at work; only He who now restrains will do so until He is taken out of the way. ⁸ And then the lawless one will be revealed, whom the Lord will consume with the breath of His mouth and destroy with **the brightness of His coming. 2 Thessalonians 2:5-8**

One of the most descriptive visions of God came from the prophet Ezekiel.

⁴ Then I looked, and behold, a whirlwind (it looked like a tornado) was coming out of the north, **a great cloud**

with raging fire engulfing itself; and brightness was all around it and radiating out of its midst like the color of amber, out of the midst of the fire...[26] And above the firmament over their heads was the likeness of a throne, in appearance like a sapphire stone; on the likeness of the throne was a likeness with the appearance of a man high above it. [27] Also from the appearance of His waist and upward I saw, as it were, **the color of amber with the appearance of fire all around within it;** and from the appearance of His waist and downward I saw, as it were, **the appearance of fire with brightness all around.** [28] Like the appearance of a rainbow in a cloud on a rainy day, **so was the appearance of the brightness all around it. This was the appearance of the likeness of the glory of the LORD.** Ezekiel 1:4, 26-28

Every time I read this description, tears well up in my eyes, I feel chills throughout my body, and I bow my head to confess my sins before the Lord God that I may not be consumed by the expressed brightness of His presence.

John, James, Peter, and Paul all saw the glory of the Lord, being eyewitness to similar visions.

[13] and in the midst of the seven lampstands One like the Son of Man, clothed with a garment down to the feet and girded about the chest with a golden band. [14] His head and hair were white like wool, as white as snow, and His eyes like a flame of fire; [15] His feet were like fine brass, as if refined in a furnace, and His voice as the sound of many waters; [16] He had in His right hand seven stars, out

of His mouth went a sharp two-edged sword, and **His countenance was like the sun shining in its strength.** **Revelation 1:13-16**

[1] Now after six days Jesus took Peter, James, and John his brother, led them up on a high mountain by themselves; [2] and He was transfigured before them. **His face shone like the sun, and His clothes became as white as the light. Matthew 17:1-2**

[12] "While thus occupied, as I journeyed to Damascus with authority and commission from the chief priests, [13] at mid-day, O king, along the road **I saw a light from heaven, brighter than the sun, shining around me** and those who journeyed with me. **Acts 26:12-13**

What was their reaction when they saw the resurrected Christ in all His glory? Did they run up to Him and hug His neck? Did they greet Him like a buddy at a dinner party?

[7] And when I saw Him, **I fell at His feet as dead. Revelation 1:17**

[6] And when the disciples heard it, **they fell on their faces and were greatly afraid. Matthew 17:6**

[14] **And when we all had fallen to the ground,** I heard a voice speaking to me and saying in the Hebrew language, 'Saul, Saul, why are you persecuting Me? It is hard for you to kick against the goads.' **Acts 26:14**

How do you react when you enter His presence?

Why did the Lord reveal His glory to the children of Israel?

¹ But now, thus says the LORD, who created you, O Jacob, and He who formed you, O Israel: "Fear not, for I have redeemed you; I have called you by your name; You are Mine. ² When you pass through the waters, I will be with you; and through the rivers, they shall not overflow you. When you walk through the fire, you shall not be burned, nor shall the flame scorch you. ³ For I am the LORD your God, the Holy One of Israel, your Savior; I gave Egypt for your ransom, Ethiopia and Seba in your place. ⁴ Since you were precious in My sight, you have been honored, and I have loved you; therefore, I will give men for you, and people for your life. ⁵ Fear not, for I am with you; I will bring your descendants from the east and gather you from the west; ⁶ I will say to the north, 'Give them up!' and to the south, 'Do not keep them back!' Bring My sons from afar, and My daughters from the ends of the earth ⁷ **Everyone who is called by My name, whom I have created for My glory**; I have formed him, yes, I have made him." **Isaiah 43:1-7**

Why did the Lord reveal His glory in the Church, the body of Christ?

³ Blessed be the God and Father of our Lord Jesus Christ, who has blessed us with every spiritual blessing in the heavenly places in Christ, ⁴ just as He chose us in Him before the foundation of the world, that we should be holy and without blame before Him in love, ⁵ having predestined us to adoption as sons by Jesus Christ to Himself, according to the good pleasure of His will, ⁶ **to the praise of the glory of His grace**, by which He made us accepted in the Beloved. **Ephesians 1:3-6**

¹³ In Him you also trusted, after you heard the word of truth, the gospel of your salvation; in whom also, having believed, you were sealed with the Holy Spirit of promise, ¹⁴ who is the guarantee of our inheritance until the redemption of the purchased possession, **to the praise of His glory. Ephesians 1:13-14**

How marvelous is the redemptive plan of our God! We were created to be held up as trophies on exhibit to the rest of creation revealing the attribute of God's grace.

15. **God is Holy.** The Lord is awesomely, gloriously, majestically holy. I feel totally inadequate to begin to describe the holiness of the Most High God. Of all the attributes of God, this is the one attribute that is used the most to describe Him. There are creatures, the Cherubim, that remain in His presence all day and night who never cease to cry out to one another, concerning the holiness of the Lord. These are the most powerful of all the angelic beings, yet they are mere servants before the Almighty.

⁸ Each of the four living creatures had six wings and was covered with eyes all around, even under its wings. Day and night they never stop saying: "'**Holy, holy, holy is the Lord God Almighty**,' who was, and is, and is to come." **Revelation 4:8**

What is the true meaning of holy as it pertains to God? The word holy means sacred, extensively set apart.

John MacArthur writes this about God's holiness:

"What is the first thing that comes to mind when you worship God? Is it His infinite wisdom, His unlimited power, or His ultimate sovereignty? Is it some attribute or characteristic you find particularly appealing, awe-inspiring, or comforting? Knowing that God is immutable, omnipotent, omnipresent, and omniscient is significant, but those attributes give limited insight into what God expects of us. What is it–beyond His unchanging, all-powerful, infinitely knowing presence that compels us to worship? It is basically this: God is holy. Of all the attributes of God, holiness is the one that most uniquely describes Him and in reality, is a summation of all His other attributes. The word holiness refers to His separateness, His otherness, the fact that He is unlike any other being. It indicates His complete and infinite perfection. Holiness is the attribute of God that binds all the others together."

All that He is, and everything that He does is holy. The only place where holiness abides is wherever God is. This means that everything God creates is created holy. Yes, humans along with all creation were created holy. Listen to the Lord describe creation after the sixth day.

31 God saw all that he had made, and it was very good. And there was evening, and there was morning the sixth day. 1 Thus the heavens and the earth were completed in all their vast array. 2 By the seventh day God had finished the work he had been doing; so on the seventh day he rested from all his work. 3 Then God blessed the seventh day and made it holy, because on it he rested from all the work of creating that he had done. **Genesis 1:31-2:3**

The seventh day was hallowed, declared holy because all that He created was very good and He completed creating all things. All things mean everything that is currently in existence and everything that has ceased to exist due to being tainted by sin. All remains to God for He is the past, present, and future.

Nothing can enter His presence without first acknowledging His holiness and second worshiping before His holy throne. We, His children, are commanded to:

[23] Sing to the LORD, all the earth; proclaim the good news of His salvation from day to day. [24] Declare His glory among the nations, His wonders among all peoples. [25] For the LORD is great and greatly to be praised; He is also to be feared above all gods. [26] For all the gods of the peoples are idols, but the LORD made the heavens. [27] Honor and majesty are before Him; strength and gladness are in His place. [28] Give to the LORD, O families of the peoples, give to the LORD glory and strength. [29] Give to the LORD the glory due His name; bring an offering, and come before Him. Oh, worship the LORD in the beauty of holiness! [30] Tremble before Him, all the earth. The world also is firmly established, it shall not be moved. [31] Let the heavens rejoice, and let the earth be glad; and let them say among the nations, "The LORD reigns."[32] Let the sea roar, and all its fullness; let the field rejoice, and all that is in it. [33] Then the trees of the woods shall rejoice before the LORD, for He is coming to judge the earth. [34] Oh, give thanks to the LORD, for He is good! For His mercy endures forever. [35] And say, "Save us, O God of our salvation; gather us together, and deliver us from the

Gentiles, to give thanks to Your holy name, to triumph in Your praise." [36] Blessed be the LORD God of Israel from everlasting to everlasting! **1 Chronicles 16:23-36**

[1] Give unto the LORD, O you mighty ones, give unto the LORD glory and strength. [2] Give unto the LORD the glory due to His name; worship the LORD in the beauty of holiness. **Psalms 29:1-2**

There is nothing further that I can add to the description, than that which the word of God provides on the holiness of our great God, Savior, and King to whom be glory, honor, worship, and praise for ever and ever. Amen!

CHAPTER 4

The Compilation of Judgment

The Detestable Abominations

Being placed in remembrance of who God is and His solemn character, we now have the proper context that enhances our understanding of how and why the Lord judges sin so severely. This is extremely important, as I cannot recall a verse in the scriptures where the Lord provided an explanation of why He did and does certain things. Nevertheless, as His attributes reveal to us God's true nature, it becomes self-evident through past activities why the Lord does certain things.

Let us resume our discussion on the judgment enacted upon Sodom and Gomorrah by examining the biblical documented behavior of the cities' residents that led to this judgment. Keep in mind that Sodom and Gomorrah were not under the Mosaic covenant or law, yet we read the following in Romans chapter 2.

² **For as many as have sinned without law will also perish without law,** and as many as have sinned in the law will be judged by the law ¹³ (for not the hearers of the law are just in the sight of God, but the doers of the law will be justified; ¹⁴ **for when Gentiles, who do not have the law, by nature do the things in the law, these, although not having the law, are a law to**

themselves, ¹⁵ who show the work of the law written in their hearts, their conscience also bearing witness, and between themselves their thoughts accusing or else excusing them) ¹⁶ in the day when God will judge the secrets of men by Jesus Christ, according to my gospel. **Romans 2:12-16**

The penalty under the Mosaic Law for such gross sin in the eyes of the Lord was physical death. Yet, a careful study of the word of God also makes clear that homosexuality was not the only issue the Lord had against the people of this region.

Region?

Yes, region.

Let's start with the prophet **Ezekiel. In the 16ᵗʰ chapter verses 48 through 50,** we read, "As I live, saith the Lord God, Sodom thy sister hath not done, she nor her daughters, as thou hast done, thou and thy daughters. Behold, this was the iniquity of thy sister Sodom, **pride, fullness of bread**, and **abundance of idleness** was in her and in her daughters, **neither did she strengthen the hand of the poor and needy.** And they were **haughty**, and **committed abomination** before me: therefore, I took them away as I saw good."

In this passage, we see the Lord providing more details regarding the judgment of Sodom and Gomorrah.

1. **Pride** – they were arrogant against the Lord; it's the original sin committed by Lucifer (Satan).

2. **Fullness of bread** – they thought, through the abundance of their own riches, that they had no need of God and were coveters.

3. **Abundance of idleness** – they were gossipers and back-biters, spreading lies in hypocrisy, plotting to do evil.

4. **Mistreated the poor and needy** – not only did they not assist the poor, they actually took advantage of the poor. They would lend knowing that the poor could not pay them back, then take even that little the poor had as collateral. The Jews in Judah were treating the poor worse than that. The law stated that you are not to take the poor's cloak (bed and clothing) for more than a "morning" (that is daylight hours) if that was used as collateral. You had to give it back during the evening so that the poor had a place to sleep and keep warm, but the rich Jews were doing the opposite. They were exploiting the poor by taking their cloaks, not giving them back and charging them interest on that which they did not have, bringing their own brothers into slavery and not releasing them for Jubilee, which was forbidden.

5. **Haughty** – they boasted openly about their sins, didn't attempt to hide it and encouraged others to participate.

6. **Last, homosexuality** – not that it was the least of all the sins brought forth by the Lord, it was not. This particular sin was by far the most egregious, as it alone on this list is called an abomination in the site of the Most Holy. This is the only sin that is described by the word of God which are the consequences when the Lord removes the restraining power of the Holy Spirit. Notice the progressive deceleration after the restraints are removed:

   a. **God gave them up to uncleanness (impurity of lustfulness).**

b. **God gave them up to vile affections (depraved passions).**

c. **God gave them over to a reprobate mind (godless immorality).**

We will discuss these in more detail later.

So, what does the Bible mean when God deems something an abomination?

I like this definition and explanation from our friends at Christian Answers:

"An abomination is something that causes hate or disgust. In biblical usage, an *abomination* is something that God loathes or hates because it is offensive to Him and His holy character."

The Hebrew words translated "abomination" are often used in association with things like idolatry and false gods.

² If a man or woman living among you in one of the towns the LORD gives you is found doing evil in the eyes of the LORD your God in violation of his covenant, ³ and contrary to my command has worshiped other gods, bowing down to them or to the sun or the moon or the stars in the sky, ⁴ and this has been brought to your attention, then you must investigate it thoroughly. If it is true and it has been proved that this detestable thing has been done in Israel, ⁵ take the man or woman who has done this evil deed to your city gate and stone that person to death. **Deuteronomy 17:2-5**

¹⁵ "Cursed is anyone who makes an idol —a thing detestable to the LORD, the work of skilled hands—and sets it up in secret." Then all the people shall say, "Amen!" **Deuteronomy 27:15**

³⁴ But they set their abominations in the house, which is called by My name, to defile it. **Jeremiah 32:34**

In **1 Kings 11:5**, the god <u>Molech</u> is called "the abomination of the Ammonites"

⁴ For it was so, when Solomon was old, that his wives turned his heart after other gods; and his heart was not loyal to the LORD his God, as was the heart of his father, David. ⁵ For Solomon went after Ashtoreth the goddess of the Sidonians, and after Milcom the abomination of the Ammonites. **1 Kings 11:4-5**

The New International Version translates it as "the detestable god of the Ammonites." The point is that God hates the falsehood, impurity, immorality, and wickedness associated with the worship of these pagan false gods.

Occult practices are also called an abomination in scripture, as is child sacrifice.

³⁵ And they built the high places of Baal which are in the Valley of the Son of Hinnom, to cause their sons and their daughters to pass through the fire to Molech, which I did not command them, nor did it come into My mind that they should do this abomination, to cause Judah to sin.' **Jeremiah 32:35**

⁹ "When you come into the land which the LORD your God is giving you, you shall not learn to follow the abominations of those nations. ¹⁰ There shall not be found among you anyone who makes his son or his daughter pass through the fire, or one who practices witchcraft, or a soothsayer, or one who interprets omens, or a sorcerer, ¹¹ or one who conjures spells, or a medium, or a spiritist, or one who calls up the dead. ¹² For all who do these

things are an abomination to the LORD, and because of these abominations the LORD your God drives them out from before you. ¹³ You shall be blameless before the LORD your God. ¹⁴ For these nations which you will dispossess listened to soothsayers and diviners; but as for you, the LORD your God has not appointed such for you. **Deuteronomy 18:9-14**

Other abominations in God's sight are ungodly sexual relationships like homosexuality, fornication, and adultery.

¹⁹ 'Also you shall not approach a woman to uncover her nakedness as long as she is in her customary impurity. ²⁰ Moreover you shall not lie carnally with your neighbor's wife, to defile yourself with her. ²¹ And you shall not let any of your descendants pass through the fire to Molech, nor shall you profane the name of your God: I am the LORD. ²² You shall not lie with a male as with a woman. It is an abomination. **Leviticus 18:19-22**

God forbid the Israelites to participate in cross-dressing.

⁵ "A woman shall not wear anything that pertains to a man, nor shall a man put on a woman's garment, for all who do so are an abomination to the LORD your God. **Deuteronomy 22:5**

One of the most important commands the Lord gave to Israel was the ordinance governing the quality of their sacrifices. They were forbidden from bringing an imperfect sacrifice. The animals that were to be offered unto the Lord must be without spot or blemish since it represented Christ.

¹ "You shall not sacrifice to the LORD your God a bull or sheep which has any blemish or defect, for that is an abomination to the LORD your God. **Deuteronomy 17:1**

Daily life was also addressed. Therefore, everyone was forbidden from dishonest business dealings.

[13] Do not have two differing weights in your bag—one heavy, one light. [14] Do not have two differing measures in your house—one large, one small. [15] You must have accurate and honest weights and measures, so that you may live long in the land the LORD your God is giving you. [16] For the LORD your God detests anyone who does these things, anyone who deals dishonestly. **Deuteronomy 25:13-16**

Most of the time, the poor were taken advantage of while the rich received discounts. This was one of the many reasons that God punished Sodom and Gomorrah.

[1] The LORD detests dishonest scales, but accurate weights find favor with him. **Proverbs 11:1**

The Lord despises overt wickedness. This is wickedness performed with pride; they enjoy their sin. People committing these types of sins have their consciences seared with a hot iron and are no longer sensitive to the law of God written on their hearts.

[9] The way of the wicked is an abomination to the LORD, but He loves him who follows righteousness. [26] The thoughts of the wicked are an abomination to the LORD, But the words of the pure are pleasant. **Proverbs 15:9, 26**

We have communicated that one of the attributes of God was justice, meaning that God is always just. In this setting, the people of Sodom and Gomorrah were guilty of injustice.

[15] He who justifies the wicked, and he who condemns the just, both of them alike are an abomination to the LORD. **Proverbs 17:15**

The rich were able to purchase influence and pervert justice while the poor had to suffer due to their inability to pay for reasonable legal defense. Moreover, the justice system was corrupt and the people rendering the judgments accepted bribes.

When sins begin to multiply unchecked, dishonesty becomes the norm, sexual immorality hits its absolute bottom, and justice is perverted. The next step is absolutely assured. The people began turning a deaf ear to God's words and instructions.

⁹ If anyone turns a deaf ear to my instruction, even their prayers are detestable. **Proverbs 28:9**

Why? Because their conscience becomes seared with a hot iron like the branding mark on cattle. They are no longer sensitive to the laws of God written on the heart. All that remains is the working of the fleshly nature, which is as wicked as its father, the devil.

You say: "I don't believe that."

Then it is quite obvious, you have not been reading the Bible, which is the word of God. There are several books in the New Testament that provides a list of wicked behaviors locked in our fleshly nature waiting to be released by our natural spirit and soul. This is the reason why God commands His children to renew our minds (soul) and subdue our flesh.

²⁸ Furthermore, just as they did not think it worthwhile to retain the knowledge of God, so God gave them over to a depraved mind, so that they do what ought not to be done. ²⁹ They have become filled with **every kind of wickedness, evil, greed and depravity. They are full of envy, murder, strife, deceit and malice. They are gossips,** ³⁰ **slanderers, God-haters, insolent,**

arrogant and boastful; they invent ways of doing evil; they disobey their parents; [31] they have no understanding, no fidelity, no love, no mercy. [32] Although they know God's righteous decree that those who do such things deserve death, they not only continue to do these very things but also approve of those who practice them. **Romans 1:28-32**

[16] So I say, walk by the Spirit, and you will not gratify the desires of the flesh. [17] For the flesh desires what is contrary to the Spirit, and the Spirit what is contrary to the flesh. They are in conflict with each other, so that you are not to do whatever you want. [18] But if you are led by the Spirit, you are not under the law. [19] **The acts of the flesh are obvious: sexual immorality, impurity and debauchery; [20] idolatry and witchcraft; hatred, discord, jealousy, fits of rage, selfish ambition, dissensions, factions [21] and envy; drunkenness, orgies, and the like.** I warn you, as I did before, that those who live like this will not inherit the kingdom of God. **Galatians 5:16-21**

There are a few additional scriptural references, but you get the picture.

The final abomination we will look at is a hypocritical offering from the unrepentant heart.

What exactly is a hypocritical offering from an unrepentant heart?

We have seen from one of His attributes, that God is holy. We also take note that God is a Spirit, which simply means He is not visible to the physical eye and does not possess a body prior to creating the angels and men. Now, of course, He resides today in the body of the man Christ Jesus the Lord. Due to the purity of His holiness, the Lord cannot by any means compromise with impurity, whether it be hidden in our hearts or overt wickedness. Anyone who has unclean hands, feet, or heart cannot approach the Holy God. For this reason, the Lord requires that a man be born again. We obtain a sin-filled heart from our natural fathers, hence contaminating everything we think, say, and do. This is unacceptable to the Lord, who is holy.

We must first be washed in the blood of the Lamb, Jesus Chris, and be cleansed from all impurities as we sojourn in this world in our fleshly bodies. Our feet become dirty from thoughts, words, and deeds. The hypocritical offering is our willingness to attempt to worship a holy God knowing that we have not accepted the prescribed method and only way the Lord has commanded us to approach Him. It is overt disobedience to a direct command of God.

CHAPTER 5

The Conclusiveness of Judgment

The main issues the Sodomites and Gomorrahrians had were that they gloated in their immorality and utterly refused to repent, to apply any measure of self-control or limitations to their debauchery. Had they repented instead of attempting to act out their fleshly sensual appetites and sexual aggression, the Lord would have spared the cities.

You may ask, "How do you know that for certain?"

Well, listen to the Lord. [23] And you, Capernaum, will you be lifted to the heavens? No, you will go down to Hades. For if the miracles that were performed in you had been performed in Sodom, it would have remained to this day. [24] But I tell you that it will be more bearable for Sodom on the day of judgment than for you." **Matthew 11:23-24**

After witnessing the record of the word of God against Sodom, Gomorrah, and the surrounding cities, do you still believe their hands and hearts were clean in God's eyes? This is not you nor I judging behavior from an external point of view; rather, it is the Lord who judges the thoughts and intents of the heart.

Listen again to the Lord's rebuke of those who attempt to come to worship Him with an unrepentant, impure, and unclean heart.

[8] The LORD detests the sacrifice (of the lips, prayer and worship) of the wicked, but the prayer of the upright pleases him. **Proverbs 15:8**

[13] Stop bringing meaningless offerings! Your incense (prayers) is detestable to me. New Moons, Sabbaths and convocations I cannot bear your worthless assemblies (church attendance). [14] Your New Moon feasts and your appointed festivals I hate with all my being. They have become a burden to me; I am weary of bearing them. [15] **When you spread out your hands in prayer, I hide my eyes from you; even when you offer many prayers, I am not listening**. Your hands are full of blood! [16] Wash and make yourselves clean. Take your evil deeds out of my sight; stop doing wrong. [17] Learn to do right; seek justice. Defend the oppressed. Take up the cause of the fatherless; plead the case of the widow. [18] "Come now, let us settle the matter," says the LORD. "Though your sins are like scarlet, they shall be as white as snow; though they are red as crimson, they shall be like wool. [19] If you are **willing and obedient**, you will eat the good things of the land; [20] but if you resist and rebel, you will be devoured by the sword." For the mouth of the LORD has spoken. **Isaiah 1:13-20**

Most of the references to that which is abominable or detestable are found in the books of Leviticus and Deuteronomy. There are many prophecies within those two books that declare God's judgment against Israel. The differences between the two biblical books are, Leviticus was given at Mount Sinai, while Deuteronomy was written thirty plus years later. The Lord had Moses expand on the laws and ordinances during the wilderness wandering, as the younger generation was preparing to enter the Promised Land. They faced situations that were not experienced during the years of wilderness wandering, as things such as borders, cities, jurisdictions, law fare, warfare, worship center, and municipalities are addressed.

Proverbs 6 contains a list of seven things that God calls abominations: "There are six things that the Lord hates, seven that are an abomination to him: haughty eyes, a lying tongue, and hands that shed innocent blood, a heart that devises wicked plans, feet that make haste to run to evil, a false witness who breathes out lies, and one who sows discord among brothers." **Proverbs 6:16–19**

In **Luke 16:15**, Jesus tells the Pharisees, "You are the ones who justify yourselves in the eyes of others, but God knows your hearts. What people value highly is detestable in God's sight."

The context of Jesus' statement is a rebuke of the Pharisees' love of money. He had just been teaching that a person cannot serve two masters and that serving God and serving money are mutually exclusive. This was happening in Sodom and Gomorrah and is certainly taking place in America today.

13 "No one can serve two masters. Either you will hate the one and love the other, or you will be devoted to the one and despise the other. You cannot serve both God and money." 14 The Pharisees, who loved money, heard all this and were sneering at Jesus. **Luke 16:13-14**

The Pharisees responded with ridicule, showing the blindness of an evil heart that revels in what God calls an abomination.

This scene is observed today in every state, city, workplace, educational institutions from kindergarten to colleges and universities, through professional programs, in most homes daily, and many churches every Sunday. The false expectations that God will bless such behavior is utterly ridiculous and delusional. Yet, almost every Sunday, the prosperity "gospel" of health and wealth is preached from pulpits and rejoiced over by parishioners with itching ears. Preach a message on holiness, godliness, and servitude to God, the next week you would lose half your members.

God is holy and separate from sinners. The Lord cannot compromise with sin; neither will He overlook sin.

"How can I speak with such certainty about this issue?" you may ask.

The cross!

Titus 1:16 says that false teachers may "claim to know God, but by their actions they deny him. They are detestable, disobedient and unfit for doing anything good."

From idolatry to unfair scales. From ungodly lewd sexual relationships to wickedness of various kinds, they are all abominations that further separate people from a Holy God. Really, all sin, which is lawlessness, as well as coming short of God's perfection and holiness, can be considered an abomination. All sin separates us further from God's presence and is detestable to Him.

[34] Righteousness exalts a nation, but sin condemns any people. **Proverbs 14:34**

⁹ The LORD detests the way of the wicked, but he loves those who pursue righteousness. **Proverbs 15:9**

Lest one think that this verse refers to righteous deeds, we must understand that Christ is being pursued.

¹⁷ I will give thanks to the LORD because of his righteousness; I will sing the praises of the name of the LORD Most High. **Psalms 7:17**

³⁰ But of him are ye in Christ Jesus, who of God is made unto us wisdom, and righteousness, and sanctification, and redemption: ³¹ That, according as it is written, He that glory, let him glory in the Lord. **1 Corinthians 1:30-31**

God's hatred of sin makes Christ's sacrifice on the cross even more astonishing. ³² He who did not spare his own Son but gave him up for us all **(Romans 8:32);** when "God made him who had no sin to be sin for us, so that in him we might **MADE THE RIGHTOUSNESS** of God". **2 Corinthians 5:21**

As He suffered and died upon the cross for our sin, Jesus is identified by the psalmist: "I am a worm and not a man, scorned by everyone, despised by the people" **Psalm 22:6**. Jesus took our abominations upon Himself and gave us the gift of His righteousness in return. All who put their trust in Him will be saved.

But hold your horses. God has even more reasons for Sodom's judgment. In **Jeremiah 23:14**, God tells the inhabitants (Jews) of Jerusalem "I have seen also in the prophets of Jerusalem a horrible thing: they **commit adultery** and **walk in lies**: they **strengthen also the hands of evildoers**, that **none doth return from his wickedness**: they are all of them unto me as Sodom, and the inhabitants thereof as Gomorrah."

Here is the list:

1. **Adultery** – most of the false gods' temples were basically prostitution houses, especially the so-called female deities. What was happening in the temples were that the married men would go there to worship the false god and eventually have sexual relations with the temple maidens who had devoted their lives to the gods.

2. **Walk in lies** – they didn't just tell lies. They lived according to those lies and caused people to rebel openly against the Most Holy. This is evident in our day; we call it propaganda. Lies are repeated so often that they are eventually told and heard as the truth.

3. **Strengthen evildoers** – the religious leaders secretly practiced sin and agreed with people committing iniquity keeping them from seeing the error of their ways and turning to the Lord through repentance. They were making their parishioners twice the child of the devil than they are. There was no justice. Again, doesn't this sound like the recent riots we witnessed here in America? Those who destroyed cities and businesses causing billions of dollars in damage were never arrested, charged, prosecuted, jailed, and forced to pay restitution. Paul said it this way in **Romans 1:32** "Who knowing the judgment of God, that they which commit such things are worthy of death, not only do the same, **but have pleasure in them that do them**."

4. **Wickedness continually** – just like the days of Noah, Sodom, and Gomorrah, the hearts of the Jews of Jeremiah's days had grown so cold towards God that they could not turn away from their evil deeds, nor did

they desire to turn away. We are now witnessing the same behavior being played out in America today. Wickedness that was once only committed in private under the cover of darkness is now paraded in our streets, celebrated by many, and promoted by those in authority. They conduct themselves in this manner as if there was no God and they hate those that honor the Most Holy.

But wait, there's more. God isn't finished. In **II Peter 2:6-7**, the Lord says; "and turning the cities of Sodom and Gomorrah into ashes condemned them with an overthrow, making them an ensample unto those that after should live ungodly; and delivered just Lot, vexed with the **filthy conversation of the wicked.**"

God says that their lifestyle was filthy. He wasn't just speaking of sensual immorality or sexual sins but depraved sensuality. Lot's daughters were married yet they were still virgins! Why? Because their husbands would rather have relations with other men than with their wives. This isn't unique to Sodom and Gomorrah; it is happening here in America today. They call it being on the "down low", that is, in secret and under the cover of darkness. They forget that God is light, and everything is done in the light in His eyes.

Finally, the Lord provides the last details of why he overthrew Sodom and Gomorrah in **Jude 7**. It reads, "Even as Sodom and Gomorrah, and the cities about them in like manner, **giving themselves over to fornication**, and **going after strange flesh**, are set forth for an example, suffering the vengeance of eternal fire."

1. **Gave themselves** – this mean that they were so totally committed to these sinful acts that there was never going

to be repentance. They were sinning with their whole heart. This is in total contrast to the psalmist who said, "with my whole heart have I sought you, let me not wander from your commands." **Psalm 119:10** and again "O how I love your word! It is my meditation all day long." **Psalm 119:97**

2. **Going after strange flesh** – they took the final step on God's immorality ladder with homosexuality, and bestiality. Most heinous of all, the men of Sodom and Gomorrah attempted to have sex with angels. These angels were sent by God to validate the sins of the people. Oh, how merciful is our God. He was giving them another opportunity to be saved instead of just instantly raining down fire and brimstone from the heavens. Once the angels saw that the people had totally surrendered themselves as slaves to their wicked passions, the angels turned their attention to saving Lot and his family because they were the only righteous people in Sodom and the surrounding cities.

This is what happens to people, cities, and nations when they "give themselves" to their destructive ungodly fleshly behavior. God's response is recorded in **Romans 1:18-32**. Notice the downward progression.

"The wrath of God is being revealed from heaven against all the godlessness and wickedness of people, who suppress the truth by their wickedness, since what may be known about God is plain to them, because God has made it plain to them. For since the creation of the world God's invisible qualities—his eternal power and divine nature—have been clearly seen, being understood from what has been made, so that *all* people are without excuse. For although they knew God, they neither glorified him as God nor gave thanks to him, but their thinking became futile, and their foolish hearts were darkened. Although they claimed to be wise, they became fools and exchanged the glory of the immortal God for images made to look like a mortal human being and birds and animals and reptiles. Therefore, **God gave them up to uncleanness,** in the sinful desires of their hearts to sexual impurity for the degrading of their bodies with one another. They exchanged the truth about God for a lie and worshiped and served created things rather than the Creator—who is forever praised. Amen. Because of this, **God gave them up to vile affections**. Even their women exchanged natural sexual relations for unnatural ones. In the same way the men also abandoned natural relations with women and were inflamed with lust for one another. Men committed shameful acts with other men and received in themselves the due penalty for their error. Furthermore, just as they did not think it worthwhile to retain the knowledge of God, so **God gave them over to a reprobate mind**, so that they do what ought not to be done. They have become **filled with every kind of wickedness, evil, greed and depravity**. They are full of envy, murder, strife, deceit, and malice. They are gossips, slanderers, God-haters, insolent, arrogant and boastful; **they invent ways of doing evil**; they disobey their parents, they have no understanding, no fidelity, no love, no mercy. Although they know God's righteous decree that those who do such things deserve death, they not only continue to do these very things but also approve of those who practice them."

1. God also *gave them up* to uncleanness – sexual immorality or impurity. The first thing that happens is there will be a sexual revolution. All the normal restraints for biblical sexual intimacy are discarded and replaced

by man's alternatives. Nudity and promiscuity replace modesty and chivalry. Marriage is despised and adultery is acceptable. Monogamy is cast aside for the swingers' club. Pornography is peddled throughout the land, even to children.

2. God *gave them up* unto vile affections – to **love** that which is immoral, unnatural, and reprehensible. Homosexuality comes out of the closet and is promoted as an alternative lifestyle.

3. God *gave them over* to a reprobate mind – a depraved and seared conscious that is set on performing every evil deed that can possibly enter the heart of a sin-filled human. This person has so given themselves over to the lust of the flesh that they will not hear God's voice even if He was standing directly in front of them with a bullhorn. That which is natural is converted to perverseness, men becoming women and women becoming men. Children being forced into participating in the moral depravity of wicked adults. God's institution of marriage between one man and one woman is mocked and scoffed at, as men attempt to marry men and women with other women. Even that which defies all logic is championed as giant leaps forward in the name of tolerance and acceptance: men being impregnated and women being able to father children. The fallout for denying God's word has left every society that has attempted to "go at it alone," destitute and impoverished.

How shall America escape?

CHAPTER 6

THE COMING JUDGMENT

The Fall of America the Beautiful

History has shown that the public acceptance of homosexuality is the final downward step in the fall of a nation. Babylon, Persia, Greece, and Rome all once ruled the world. All have fallen when this behavior became popular with the leaders and the general public. God has not and will never change. He is Holy and will judge sin, His holiness demands that He judge sin. The Lord has also declared that He will not be mocked, that whatsoever a man sows that he shall also reap. If we sow wickedness, we will reap evil. If we sow righteousness, we will reap peace and prosperity.

My heart cries out for mercy as the wrath of God is imminent upon America if we do not repent and cry out to Him like the city of Nineveh at the preaching of Jonah.

Let us take a walk down history lane to determine if America is on the path of righteousness or the path of destruction.

The timeline below is from Robert Clifton Robinson's essay titled The Stunning Evidence Of America's Moral Decline BY ROB ROBINSON *on* NOVEMBER 2, 2020

"A Timeline Illustrating the Moral Decline of the United States"

Our abandonment of God, as a nation and people, began in 1962 when prayer in school came under criticism.[30]

1962: The end of school prayer. In Engle v. Vitale, the Supreme Court reinterpreted the First Amendment's protection of religion as a right of free exercise because of complaints from parents. The following is the prayer that parents objected to: "Almighty God, we acknowledge our dependence upon Thee, and we beg Thy blessings upon us, our parents, our teachers and our country. Amen."[31]

1962: A change in the national abortion law is advocated by the American Law Institute.

1963: The national debt for the United States is $306 million dollars, the gross domestic product is $645 million. In 2015, the national debt will grow to over 18 trillion dollars.

1963: A lower court rules that the Bible is no longer allowed in public schools. In Abington v. Schempp, the court determines that no school board or state law has the right to require students to read Bible scriptures at the start of the school day.

1963: The Supreme Court rules that prayer is not allowed in school. Madalyn Murray O'Hair founds "The American Atheists." In Murray v. Curlett, the Supreme Court rules 8 to 1 in favor of abolishing school prayer and Bible reading in public schools.

1965: Homosexual activists picket the White House and Pentagon. In San Francisco, gay activists conduct the first gay drag ball. The first gay community center opens in San Francisco.

1965: Griswold v. Connecticut; the U.S. Supreme Court establishes that the U.S. Constitution guarantees homosexuals the right to privacy, though this right is not explicitly stated in the Constitution.

1966: *Time* magazine declares "God is Dead."

1967: The first gay campus group is formed at Columbia College in New York City.

1967: The Summer of Love begins in San Francisco. One hundred thousand young people celebrate free love with no regard for the consequences.

1967: The addition of sociology and social psychology curriculum is placed into public schools.

1969: A Gallup poll reveals that 68% of Americans believe premarital sex is wrong and 21% said it is not. In 2009, 40 years later, 32% stated that premarital sex is wrong and 60% declared that it is socially acceptable.

1972: The topic of abortion is discussed on the sitcom, Maude; Maude Findlay has an abortion.

1973: Feminist leader Gloria Steinem declares, "By the year 2000, we will, I hope, raise our children to believe in human potential, not God."

1973: In the Supreme Court decision, Roe v. Wade, abortion becomes legal in all states.

1976: Parents and spouses are no longer included in the decision to have a baby aborted. Any teenager may have an abortion without the knowledge or approval of their parents. A wife may abort her baby without her husband's approval.

1976: The Hyde Amendment prohibits the use of federal funds to pay for abortions.

1977: The Hyde Amendment is amended due to objections from the American Civil Liberties Union, to include pregnancies that are the result of rape or incest.

1980: In Stone v. Graham, the Ten Commandments are no longer allowed in any state or federal building.

1981: Arkansas passes a law requiring that creation must be taught alongside evolution in public schools. The Supreme Court determines that this law is unconstitutional. Only evolution is taught in public schools.

1984: The first domestic partner law is enacted in Berkeley, California.

1986: California grants the first lesbian couple joint adoption rights.

1986: All restrictions on abortion are removed in a majority decision: Thornburg v. American College of Obstetricians and Gynecologists.

We kill millions of unborn children each year for the sake of convenience or as an irresponsible form of birth control.[32] Only one in ten of all abortions performed worldwide are done to save the life of the mother or in the case of a rape.[33] The other nine children are murdered for the sake of convenience because of the selfishness and sinful acts of human beings.

1987: The Gay and Lesbian Caucus of the National Education Association is established.

1987: The life of Jesus Christ is mocked in the movie, *The Last Temptation of Christ.* Martin Scorsese receives an Oscar nomination for Best Director.

1989: Seinfeld airs for the first time on NBC. This television production has a dramatic impact on American culture. The primary theme of Seinfeld defines human life as meaningless or irrational. The characters on Seinfeld have little regard for issues of morality.

1989: Denmark is the first country to legalize same-sex marriage.

1991: The first lesbian kiss is seen on network television.

1992: The Supreme Court rules that a graduation prayer violates the "Establishment Clause" of the Constitution. This was that prayer: "O God, we are grateful for the learning which we have celebrated on this joyous commencement ... we give thanks to you, Lord, for keeping us alive, sustaining us and allowing us to reach this special, happy occasion."

1993: The first laws are enacted that protect lesbian, gay, bisexual, and transgender (LGBT) students in public schools.

1994: The first school prom for gays is held in Los Angeles.

1995: National Police in Manila, Philippines discover a plot by Ramzi Yousef to blow up a dozen U.S. airliners while they are flying over the Pacific.

1995: April 19, Timothy McVeigh kills 168 people and wounds 680, by use of a domestic terrorist bomb attack on the Alfred P. Murrah Federal Building in downtown Oklahoma City.

1997: Ellen DeGeneres "comes out" publicly as a lesbian in an appearance on The Oprah Winfrey Show. She later appears on the cover of *Time* magazine.

1997: Bill Clinton is the first U.S. president to address a gay organization during the Human Rights Campaign.

1997: New Hampshire and Maine enact gay rights laws.

1998: Will and Grace premiers on NBC, which features two homosexuals with frequent references to gay sex.

1998: Osama Bin Laden issues a "fatwa," commanding every Muslim to kill Americans, both military and civilian, wherever they can be found in the world.

1998: America's president, Bill Clinton, has sex in the oval office with Monica Lewinski. Many other affairs are discovered, yet he leaves office with a 65% approval rating.

1999: April 20, Columbine High School massacre. Two high school seniors—Dylan Klebold and Eric Harris—kill 12 students, 1 teacher, and themselves; 21 are injured.

2000: Vermont passes HB847, legalizing civil unions for same-sex couples.

2000: Al-Qaeda uses a motorboat in Yemen, filled with explosives, to blow a hole in the side of the USS *Cole*, killing seventeen American sailors.

2000: George W. Bush is elected the forty-third president of the United States and takes office in January 2001.

2001: Al-Qaeda terrorists attack the Twin Towers in New York City, killing 2,977 Americans, by hijacking four fully fueled jetliners. The United States government launches the "War on Terror."

2003: Lawrence v. Texas, the Supreme Court voids state sodomy laws by extension and invalidates sodomy laws in thirteen other states, making same-sex activity legal in every U.S. state and territory.

2003: Renee Doyle, president of "EdWatch"; The National Institute of Mental Health; and the National Science Foundation announces "religious traditionalists are mentally disturbed."

2005: Hurricane Katrina kills 1,833 people, in one of the deadliest storms in U.S. History.

2006: Richard Dawkins, "atheist with a mission," attacks Christianity in his book, *The God Delusion.*

2008: Barack Hussein Obama is elected the first black president of the United States. He was the most liberal member of Congress in the history of the United States.

2008: The national debt of the United States is $10 billion, 25 million; the GDP is $14 billion, 843 million.

2009: A Gallop poll reveals that just 32% say premarital sex is wrong and 60% say that sexual relationships between consenting adults—married or not—is acceptable.

2009: *Newsweek* magazine announces "The Decline and Fall of Christian America" on its cover. *Newsweek,* April 14, "The End of Christian America."

2009: A Rasmussen report describes 88% of Americans believers in the person known in history as Jesus Christ. 82%

believe Jesus Christ is the Son of God who came to earth and died for our sins. 79% of Americans believe that Jesus rose from the dead. Despite claims to follow Christ, Christians do not go to the voting booths and support the issues that those who believe the Bible should endorse.

2010: A record of 44.7 million people receive food stamps.

2011: National Campaign to Prevent Teen and Unplanned Pregnancy reports that 80% of evangelical Christians, from the age of twenty to twenty-nine, have had premarital sex.

2012: Vice-president of the United States, Joe Biden, endorses same-sex marriage in an interview on NBC's Meet the Press.

2012: Barack Obama becomes the first president in United States history to openly support all forms of homosexuality, gay rights, gay adoptions, and civil unions.

2012: Democrats remove God from their party platform as well as all references to God during the 2012 Democratic National Convention.

2012: July 20, a mass shooting by James Holmes occurs inside the Century movie theater in Aurora, Colorado, killing 12 people and injuring 70 others.

2012: Hurricane Sandy is the second most costly storm in U.S. History, at 68 billion dollars; 285 people died.

2012: December 14, Adam Lanza kills 20 school children and 6 adults at the Sandy Hook Elementary School in Newtown, Connecticut, in the deadliest school shooting in U.S. history.

2014: The national debt grows beyond $18 trillion on December 15, 2014. The nation's debt is now greater than the economic output of the entire country.

2015: June 26, The Supreme Court of the United States makes same-sex marriage legal in all 50 states.

2015: Obergefell v. Hodges, 576 U.S., the Supreme Court rules that the fundamental right to marry is guaranteed to same-sex couples by both the Due Process Clause and the Equal Protection Clause of the Fourteenth Amendment to the United States Constitution.

2015: October 1, Christopher Harper-Mercer, a 26-year-old enrolled at the school, fatally shoots an assistant professor and 9 students in a classroom; 9 others are also injured. After the shooter is wounded, he commits suicide by shooting himself in the head. This is the deadliest mass shooting in Oregon's modern history.

2015: December 2, Syed Rizwan Farook and Tashfeen Malik, a married couple living in the city of Redlands, kill 16 people, and seriously injure 19 in a terrorist attack in San Bernardino, California. Farook is an American-born U.S. Citizen. Malik is a Pakistani-born lawful permanent resident of the United States.

2015: June 28, the national debt of the United States is 18 trillion, 284 billion. The gross domestic product is 16.77 trillion.

In the year 2015, there are 325 deaths by mass shooting. Source: Gun Violence Archives.[34]

It is important to notice the increasing natural disasters, national debt, and attacks by enemies—foreign and domestic—as America's morality, corruption, and disregard for God increases.

2016: June 12, Omar Mateen kills 49 people and injures 58 members of the LGBT community at the Pulse nightclub.

2016: November, Donald Trump is elected president of the United States, Mike Pence, vice president.

2016: Dozens are killed in Oakland Warehouse Fire.

2017: Fort Lauderdale airport shooting. Hollywood International Airport in Broward County, Florida, on January 6, 2017, near the baggage claim in Terminal 2. Five people are killed, six others injured. Approximately 36 people are injured during the resulting panic.

2017: January, Donald Trump becomes the 45th president of the United States, Mike Pence, vice president. The opposition Democrat party begins investigation into Trump collusion with Russia, later proven a hoax, fabricated by people seeking to remove President Trump from office.

2017: May, President Trump fires FBI director James Comey, starting the Mueller investigation.

2017: Relations between the U.S. and the U.N. and North Korea strain after the country tests missiles in various places.

2017: August, Hurricane Harvey makes landfall in the United States, flooding broad swaths of Texas and Louisiana and causing tens of billions of dollars of damage, making it one of the costliest natural disasters in U.S. history.

2017: September, Hurricane Irma makes landfall in Florida and causes tens of billions of dollars in damage. Irma also wrecks many Caribbean Islands.

2017: September, Hurricane Maria makes landfall on Puerto Rico as a category five hurricane, killing hundreds and knocking out the island's power.

2017: October, A gunman opens fire at a Las Vegas Strip during an outdoor concert, killing 58 people and injuring 546. This is the deadliest mass shooting in modern U.S. history.

2017: November, gunman Devin Patrick Kelley kills 26 people and wounds 20 others before killing himself. This is the deadliest mass shooting in Texas history and the deadliest shooting in an American place of worship in modern history.

2018: February, A gunman kills 17 people and injures 17 at Marjory Stoneman Douglas High School in Parkland, Florida.

2018: January, transgender individuals are allowed to join the United States military.

2019: January, Pete Buttigieg becomes the first openly gay presidential candidate from a major political party.

2019: January 25th, the longest government shutdown in American history (December 22nd, 2018-January 25th, 2019), 35 days.

2019: January 30th, a large portion of the United States is struck by a polar vortex. The city of Chicago reaches a record low temperature of 27 degrees below zero. This continues for 52 straight hours.

2019: February 22nd, singer R. Kelly is charged with ten counts of aggravated criminal sexual abuse for incidents taking place from 1998.

2019: April 27, A gunman kills one and injures three in a California synagogue. The suspect is white supremacist John Timothy Earnest, 19 years old at the time.

2019: May 31, a city employee for Virginia Beach enters a municipal building with a gun and kills 12 people.

2019: June 14, one person dies and two more are injured after a gunman enters a Costco in Southern California.

2019: August 3, 23 people are killed and another 23 are injured in a mass shooting at a Walmart in El Paso, Texas.

2019: August 4, a gunman opens fire on a bar in Dayton, Ohio, killing nine people and injuring another 27.

2019: August 10, financier and convicted sex offender, Jeffrey Epstein, is found dead in his prison cell under mysterious circumstances. His death is declared a suicide by hanging, although the ruling is widely disputed.

2019: September 24, Speaker of the House Nancy Pelosi announces the House of Representatives will begin an impeachment inquiry against Donald Trump. After 48 million dollars, and nearly two years, President Trump is not found to have violated any laws.

2019: December 18, the U.S. House of Representatives impeaches President Donald J. Trump for high crimes and misdemeanors, though no evidence is ever presented by the Democrat members that any crime had been committed.

2020: January 21, the first patient in the United States is diagnosed with COVID-19.

2020: February 5, by a majority vote, the United States Senate acquits Donald Trump of charges related to the Trump-Ukraine scandal.

2020: March 11, the COVID-19 is declared a global pandemic, leading to a global shutdown.

2020: February 26, six people are killed in a mass shooting in Milwaukee, Wisconsin, before the perpetrator kills himself.

2020: May 25, George Floyd, an African American man living in Minneapolis, is killed during an arrest. Subsequently, protests and riots ensue.

2020: June 15, in the case Bostock v. Clayton County, the Supreme Court rules 6-3 that Title VII of the Civil Rights Act of 1964 prohibit employment discrimination against LGBTQ people, on the grounds that any such discrimination must necessarily be based on the sex of the victim, which is expressly prohibited by the statute.

2020: October 2, President Donald Trump and First Lady Melania Trump are diagnosed with COVID-19. The president is taken to Walter Reed hospital on Friday, October 2, 2020. President Trump fully recovers in just three days and leaves Walter Reed hospital on Monday, October 5, 2020. The president was treated with eight drugs: Dexamethasone, Remdesivir, Regeneron, Zinc, Vitamin D, Famotidine, Aspirin.

2020: November 2, 2020, 01:58 GMT: United States coronavirus cases: 46,809,252, deaths: 1,205,194, recovered: 33,749,374.36

2020: Presidential election, November 3, 2020 (Update posted after the results).

"If we follow the chain of events from 1962 to 2020, we see a gradual departure from conservative moral values upon which the United States was founded, to a progressive political and moral set of values. This change precipitated a marked decline in the quality of life for all Americans, and began a gradual increase in violent gun crimes, increase in immorality, and led to a global pandemic that affected America much greater than any other nation.

Why would we expect God to protect our nation from terrorists, violence, and a global pandemic when we have repeatedly stated that we don't want Him in our public schools, our government, and our personal lives?

Our children cannot pray in school. The Ten Commandments have been systematically removed from all government buildings. We have killed more than 62 million unborn since 1973, for the sake of convenience. We accept that people may live perverse lifestyles that deteriorate and diminish the institution of marriage, which was created by God, in order to be tolerant and politically correct. We say nothing, do nothing, because we don't want to be seen as hateful or prejudiced.

The Parallel Between Israel and America

There is a stunning similarity between the birth of Israel as a nation and the birth of the United States. It is certain that had the United States not come into being and become a strong supporter of Israel before 1948, Israel would not have been able to come back into their own land and become a nation once again after 2,000 years.

Israel and the United States were set apart by the Lord to be His special people. Israel was chosen to be the line of descendants who would bring the Messiah into the world. America was chosen by God to be the people who would spread the good news of the Messiah's arrival and offer salvation to all people.

It is interesting that after the death of King David, the nation of Israel was split into two nations: Israel in the south; and Judah in the north, including the city of Jerusalem.

After only 200 years the nation of Israel was divided and fell to foreign enemies. Judah followed 290 years later, when Nebuchadnezzar took the nation captive.

The United States is following the precise same course of Israel, and we have only been in existence for 244 years.

40 is the number of judgment. 6 is the number of man, incomplete, lacking. 40 X 6 = 240

The United States, in entering its 245th year as a nation." By Rob Robinson

As a nation, we must do what Nineveh did when Jonah preached the imminent judgment of God upon a sin-laden people. The whole city and region repented beginning with the king, and asked God for mercy. In response, God did not destroy the city because they all became believers. Of course, this really ticked Jonah off but that's another story. America's leaders, as well as the people, must truly repent and turn from our wicked ways and turn back to the living God.

Or like Nineveh, after those who repented died, they returned to their wicked ways, in the days when Nahum preached the imminent judgment of God 150 years later. They did not repent, and God sent forth judgment destroying the city and surrounding areas with a great overthrow. None escaped as every man, woman, child, and animal were killed by the Babylonians. Two entire books of the Bible, Jonah and Nahum, are dedicated to the revival (Jonah) and judgment (Nahum) of a wicked nation, Assyria starring its empire capital city, Nineveh.

Why would the Lord God go to this extreme to tell us about Nineveh?

Because He is merciful, compassionate, patient, of great kindness, and longsuffering, not willing that any would perish but that all come to repentance.

How can America escape, as our sins are far greater and more extensive than that of Nineveh?

We not only commit iniquity but promote it and force it upon the entire world through our wealth (financial aid and military protection). What's worst is the amount of light (knowledge of God's word) America has been exposed to since her birth. No other country, aside from Israel and maybe England, has been exposed to as much revelation of the one true God as America. This is scary folks and my heart shivers at the thought of the impending judgment that will befall America for her sins against the Most High God. For it is a fearful thing to fall into the hand of the living God who is Holy!

In your wrath, O Lord, righteous, just, and true, remember mercy. For who can stand before You if Your wrath is kindled but a little? Help us to repent of our transgressions against You, turning from our wicked ways to faith in Jesus, Your son, in hope, Father, that You will relent from Your great wrath. Open the eyes and ears of this people, that we may hear and perceive that You take no delight in the judgment of the wicked but seek reconciliation with all men. Nevertheless, O Lord God, you are Holy. Remember, I pray, Holy Father, the cross. Remember the precious blood of Your Son, whom You sent to be a propitiation for our sins and not for ours only but for the sins of the entire world. O Lord revive, O Lord restore, O Lord renew, forgive our transgressions, iniquity, and sins. Forsake not, I pray Holy Father, the works of Your hands for Your servant and Your child is called by thy name. In Jesus name I pray, amen.

The End!

ABOUT THE AUTHOR

Kevin Madison is an author, husband, and father who has walked faithfully with the Lord for over 28 years. He is the son of the late Pastor Leroy Phillips and Billie Mae Phillips, who raised their 13 children to love and fear the God of salvation and King of righteousness.

Modeling his study pattern after his former pastor, Carl Brown of Baton Rouge, LA, and current favorite pastors, Dr. John Barnett and John MacArthur, Kevin has become proficient at dissecting the scriptures verse by verse. Greatly impacted by his affection and love for the late Dr. J. Vernon McGee, who always challenged his listeners to study the entire word of God, Kevin has written many topical articles and yet to be published verse by verse commentaries on the Old Testament prophets. He is the author of several books, including *Predestined to Hell?—Why would a God of Love Consign People to Hell FOREVER?*, *The Chastisement of the Lord—How the Lord responds when Christians Sin?*, and *The God Who Loves and Hates—The Book of Obadiah—Why God loved Jacob and hated Esau*. Several other upcoming titles are soon to be published, including the much-anticipated title, *Story of the Ages—God's Plan to Eliminate the Possibility of Sin*.

NOTES

The timeline is from Robert Clifton Robinson's essay titled The Stunning Evidence of America's Moral Decline BY <u>ROB ROBINSON</u> *on* <u>NOVEMBER 2, 2020</u>

"A Timeline Illustrating the Moral Decline of the United States"

(The source of this information is author and Bible teacher Robert Clifton Robinson from his website at: <u>http://www.robertcliftonrobinson.com</u>. This work came from the Amazon ebooks: "The Prophecies of the Messiah," 2013; "Yeshu," 2013; "A Universe from God," 2014; "Only Perfect People Go to Heaven," 2015; Brutal Cross, "Glorious Resurrection," 2015; "The Suffering Servant," 2015; "The Parables, Prophecies and Prayers of Jesus," 2015. A copyright for this work is on file with the United States Copyright office, Library of Congress, 101 Independence Avenue, SE, Washington, DC. All Rights Reserved.")

John MacArthur, Grace to You
(Adapted from *Worship: The Ultimate Priority.*)
Available online at: https://www.gty.org/library/Blog/B160808
copyright ©2021 Grace to You

All scripture references are from:

**King James Version (KJV),
New King James Version (NKJV)**

Publisher: Thomas Nelson

Copyright: All rights reserved

Build date: Tuesday, March 5, 2019

New International Version (NIV)

Publisher: Biblica

Copyright: © 1973, 1978, 1984, 2011 by Biblica, Inc.

Build date: Wednesday, October 23, 2019

English Standard Version (ESV)

Publisher: Crossway

CPSIA information can be obtained
at www.ICGtesting.com
Printed in the USA
BVHW041643250122
627124BV00016B/1104